What Every Manager Needs to Know About Sexual Harassment

What Every Manager Needs to Know About Sexual Harassment

DARLENE ORLOV
MICHAEL T. ROUMELL

AMACOM

American Management Association

New York • Atlanta • Boston • Chicago • Kansas City • San Francisco • Washington, D.C.
• Brussels • Mexico City • Tokyo • Toronto

This book is available at a special
discount when ordered in bulk quantities.
For information, contact Special Sales Department,
AMACOM, an imprint of AMA Publications, a division of
American Management Association,
1601 Broadway, New York, NY 10019.

This publication is designed to provide accurate and authoritative
information in regard to the subject matter covered. It is sold with the understanding that the publisher is not engaged in rendering legal, accounting, or
other professional service. If legal advice or other expert assistance is
required, the services of a competent professional person should be sought.

Orlov, Darlene.
    What every manager needs to know about sexual harassment /
    Darlene Orlov, Michael T. Roumell.
        p.   cm.
    Includes bibliographical references and index.
    ISBN 0-8144-0492-8
    1. Sexual Harassment—Prevention—Handbooks, manuals, etc.
    2. Sexual Harassment—Law and legislation—United States
    I. Roumell, Michael T.   II. Title.
    HF5549.5.S45075   1999
        658.3'145—dc21   99–17093
                                                                  CIP

Printing number

10 9 8 7 6 5 4 3 2 1

For my parents, Evelyn and Sol Orlov,
with love and admiration.
—D.O.

To my father, The Honorable Judge Thomas Roumell,
whose wisdom and achievements taught me to persevere.
—M.T.R.

Contents

Preface

Well over half of the average adult's waking hours are spent on the job, and so it will come as no surprise that dealing with a multitude of coworker personalities can be one of life's greatest challenges. In "the old days," the office was often not only a place to earn a living, but a place to socialize, make friends, and engage in harmless gossip. In today's world, however, the workplace is a far more dangerous place. Jokes, gossip, and seemingly harmless banter can, and will, kick you in the pants if you arrive unprepared.

Among the perils of the workplace is one of the most challenging yet least understood hazards: sexual harassment. In the few years from Anita Hill to Paula Jones, the sexual harassment road has been well traveled, becoming the pinnacle of employment-related lawsuits. According to the Equal Employment Opportunity Commission (EEOC), the federal watchdog agency for employment discrimination, there has been a 42 percent increase in the number of sex discrimination claims filed from 1990 to 1997, and the number of claims specifically alleging sexual harassment has more than doubled. Companies defending these claims can spend thousands of dollars in legal fees before they ever get to court. And the stakes get higher when you consider that a sexual harassment case can cost a bundle in lost time, lower employee morale, and unwanted publicity.

As a manager in any business, you need to understand what sexual harassment is about. You don't want to be caught off guard when one of your employees comes barreling into your office with claims that the mail clerk grabbed her breast. You don't want to be tongue-tied and break into a sweat when the vice president of the company starts leaving gifts on your desk and keeps asking you to fly with her to Monaco for the weekend. You need to know what to do and how to do it. You need to know the answer to all of the following questions:

- What does sexual harassment really mean?

- How do you recognize it?

- Can you say anything about sex at the office anymore?

- Can you or should you date a coworker?

- How do you prevent sexual harassment?

- How do you stop it when you find out it's happening?

- Should you have a written policy?

- How should you train your staff?

- What do you do when someone complains to you about sexual harassment?

- Who at the company should become involved?

- How do you investigate complaints?

- How do you discipline someone who has committed an act of sexual harassment?

- What about the alleged victim?

- What do you tell other employees at the company?

- Can you as a manager be held personally responsible for sexual harassment and get stuck with a big court judgment?

- Can a man sexually harass another man?

- What if a customer complains about one of your employees?

- When should you get a lawyer involved?

And these are just a start. The questions about sexual harassment are seemingly endless, and if you, as a manager, have trouble answering even one of them, then this book is for you.

The chapter summaries in this Preface and the full chapters that follow will guide you through the sexual harassment maze while helping you to maintain your sanity. Each chapter highlights some of the important points with a true-and-false test near the beginning so that you can test your knowledge and find out what you learned at the end. Each chapter also includes case scenarios, and some offer checklists for a quick reference guide. Although the task may look daunting, we hope that reading this book will give you the confidence to deal effectively with the perils of sexual harassment.

Chapter 1: "I Know It When I See It"—The Meaning of Sexual Harassment. In the mid-1960s, the U.S. Supreme Court was grappling with a slew of pornography cases and attempted to devise a universally accepted definition of the term. "What is pornography?" the justices asked themselves. Justice Potter Stewart cut to the chase in *Jacobellis v. Ohio* with what has become one of the most famous, and perhaps most cherished, quotes in Supreme Court history. Justice Stewart defined pornography very simply: "I know it when I see it."

Defining sexual harassment may be equally as troublesome. When the unwary manager hears terms like *quid pro quo, hostile environment, severe and pervasive,* and *unwelcome sexual advances,* he or she is often confused, particularly when the courts have done a fairly poor job of developing easily understood standards. The same is true when it comes to defending against a sexual harassment claim. Isn't just telling someone to stop enough to end the matter? In many cases, the answer is no.

Chapter 1 defines the terminology and gives some real-world examples of what constitutes sexual harassment without all the legal gibberish. You will learn how to recognize and identify the various types of sexual harassment, from the obvious to the subtle, even before an incident has been reported. You will learn how to recognize behaviors that themselves may not constitute sexual harassment, but may still be inappropriate and could lead to an explosive situation in your workplace. You will learn if you have any defenses to a sexual harassment complaint, what *strict liability* means, and how strict it really is. You will learn how to handle the ten most dangerous personality types in your company and what to do when they come knocking on your door. Finally, you will learn how to turn common sense into perhaps your most valuable weapon against sexual harassment in the workplace. In essence, you *will* "know it when you see it" after reading this chapter.

Chapter 2: "When It's Important, Write It Down!"—Implementing an Effective Sexual Harassment Prevention Policy. Despite all the court decisions and media attention about sexual harassment over the past several years, it is shocking that even some fairly large companies do not have a comprehensive, understandable policy against sexual harassment. Loose, verbal policies do not suffice. The courts and the EEOC have made it clear that when a sexual harassment claim is filed, the first line of defense is a written policy showing that the employer had a sexual harassment prevention program in place. Chapter 2 sets out specific guidelines, checklists, and instructions on how to write and implement a clear, concise sexual harassment prevention policy.

You will learn about the sexual harassment policy "top ten" list, which covers the ten most important components that should be in every policy. You will learn how to develop the best possible policy by following the three declarations of war against sexual harassment: "written, accurate, and readable." Instructions on how to get the message out to the entire workforce and proper follow-up actions are also discussed. You will even be given an example of a comprehensive and effective sexual harassment prevention policy that incorporates the "top ten" list and does more than pay lip service to the topic or merely recite the statutory definitions.

This chapter introduces the concept of zero tolerance for any inappropriate conduct of a sexual nature, whether or not it rises to the level of sexual harassment in the legal sense. Anything less will put you and your company at risk. As a manager, you have to be firm and articulate on the subject of sexual harassment, or your employees will not take you seriously and troubles will abound.

This chapter will also teach you how to take a strong stand against retaliation and how to incorporate a statement to that effect in your policy. You will learn how to build trust among your workforce and alleviate any fears, real or perceived, that an employee who complains could be subject to reprisals on the job or any other adverse treatment.

Finally, you will learn how to disseminate a sexual harassment policy to your workforce and make sure everyone reads it. You will learn how burying a sexual harassment policy among scores of other workplace rules in an employee manual or handbook can be the death knell when claims surface. Although other policies and work rules are important, a written sexual harassment policy is one of those few that should be singled out, posted, and repeatedly trumpeted on a regular basis. This chapter sets the ground rules that need to be followed whenever sexual harassment raises its ugly head.

Chapter 3: "The Road to Hell Is Paved With Good Intentions"—Dealing With Your Own Personal Attitudes and Conduct. All managers need to become aware of their own biases, stereotypes, and other shortcomings. In this regard, Chapter 3 will hone in on your own beliefs about sexual harassment, the way you deal with your employees, and how others may perceive your words and actions. As a manager, you need to set the example and create an appropriate environment at your workplace. If you are perceived as not taking sexual harassment seriously, don't expect your coworkers or subordinates to do so either.

You may say, "Who me? I'd never sexually harass anyone!" But you can't avoid bringing your attitudes, beliefs, life experiences, and family background to work with you every morning. Sometimes these unavoidable traits can be misinterpreted. Seemingly innocent chatter with the receptionist about whether she's "heard the one about the naked go-go dancer" may be perfectly appropriate in some settings, but it also may set the tone for how your employees react to sexual harassment in general. You will learn how to monitor and change your behavior, if necessary, keeping in mind that you could be the accused.

This chapter also addresses your behaviors outside the office. Business trips, vendor or customer meetings, after-hour social events, and other activities are all part of the "extended workplace," where sexual harassment might come knocking. You will learn how to avoid and react to sexual harassment complaints in these settings. You will also learn how to deal with the myths of the corporate culture and how treating the customer as king can get you into trouble. Advice on handling office romances and the "love-struck" subordinate is also included in this chapter.

Finally, Chapter 3 sets out for managers the tools needed to avoid sexual harassment problems by recognizing personal behaviors and learning to treat employees and coworkers with respect and dignity in every situation.

Chapter 4: "Tell Me Your Troubles"—Taking In the Initial Complaint of Sexual Harassment. When someone complains to you about "inappropriate" behavior, all your knowledge is finally put to the test. The employee may not say the words *sexual harassment,* and the conduct being described sounds murky at best, but you smell a rat.

Chapter 4 is a practical guide to taking in a complaint of sexual harassment. You will learn when and how to do it, and whether the complaint is really about sexual harassment or something else. What if you observe behavior that you think is sexual harassment, but nobody complains? What happens when the alleged victim wants no investigation or refuses to cooperate? After reading this chapter, you'll know what to do and what can happen if you don't do the right thing. You will also be given checklists on the do's and don'ts of taking in a complaint and pointers on how to handle the ten most difficult types of complaining employees.

This chapter will teach you how to project the right image to the complaining employee and make the proper assurances about no retaliation and confidentiality. How to improve your listening skills, your demeanor, and your reactions to what you hear are covered, so the complaining employee will know that you are taking the complaint seriously and are committed to eradicating sexual harassment from the workplace.

As the intake person for a sexual harassment complaint, you represent the complaining employee's first impression of the company's sexual harassment prevention policy, and you alone will set the tone for how a possible investigation will proceed. You may also become the company's first line of defense and a star witness if the situation escalates and a lawsuit is filed. Accurate written notes, an elephant's memory, and asking the right questions are all a must.

Chapter 5: "Sherlock Holmes, Detective Clouseau, and Lieutenant Columbo All at Work"—Investigating Complaints of Sexual Harassment. The investigation process is the most important aspect of any sexual harassment complaint. This chapter is a step-by-step guide on how to do it. The EEOC, the judge, and the jurors will scrutinize and study your investigation procedures carefully.

Playing detective and conducting a proper investigation of a sexual harassment complaint is probably the hardest job that any manager faces when dealing with the issue. It is also one of the most important jobs because if the investigation is faulty, the alleged victim may suffer a wrong that was never made right and the alleged harasser may escape the punishment that he or she deserves.

At the forefront of this discussion is a company's legal obligation to investigate promptly. In other words, immediately! Sitting on an employee's complaint for a week before beginning your investigation will only make some lawyer very rich when having to defend your lax and untimely response in court. You will learn that your search for the truth may not always lead to a concrete conclusion and that the results of your investigation are not necessarily the gospel. Pointers on how to tell if someone is lying and the right questions to ask to find out are covered in this chapter.

Who should be chosen to be the detective? Should it always be you or your management staff? Should a lawyer or a professional consultant be called in to assist with the investigation? How do you even begin? This chapter reveals the answers to these important questions. You will also find out about the basic duties of an investigator, with a list of the ten most important things every investigator needs to know and a checklist of the basic don'ts when it comes to playing Sherlock Holmes.

You will also learn how and when to do witness interviews, the right questions to ask to get all the details, and what questions not to ask. You will be privy to well-honed techniques for conducting interviews with the alleged victim and how to approach the accused harasser. Follow-up interviews, interviewing additional witnesses who were not directly involved, obtaining evidence from other sources, and maintaining confidentiality are covered. Finally, you will learn how to prepare an accurate report of your findings and what to do with it once it is completed.

Chapter 6: "A Slap on the Wrist or a Kick in the Pants?"—Taking Prompt and Effective Corrective Action. Chapter 6 focuses on the second most important aspect of implementing an effective sexual harassment prevention program: prompt corrective action. Once you have concluded a sexual harassment investigation and decided that an alleged harasser is guilty, you are obligated by law to take action immediately. And this means do it now, not tomorrow or two weeks from now. Deciding what to do and actually implementing your decision is a tough assignment. You need to know what action to take, if any, when the sexual harassment investigation is inconclusive, when no sexual harassment is found, and when the results spell out *sexual harassment* in capital letters.

This chapter will teach you how to identify the options for discipline and make the punishment fit the crime for a person who engages in sexual harassment. You will learn that the victim needs attention too, and this chapter will teach you how to deal with any accommodations that the victim may need to alleviate the effects of sexual harassment. You will be given guidance on confidentiality issues and how to communicate your decision to the harasser, the alleged victim, and other employees who will have undoubtedly heard about the situation through the grapevine. Appropriate follow-up procedures to ensure that sexual harassment is stopped dead in its tracks and how to ensure that a victim is not subject to any real or perceived retaliation will also be explored.

Finally, Chapter 6 offers some insights into how the harasser can fight back with legal actions against the company. You will learn how to avoid falling into the harasser's trap and how to protect yourself and your company from legal liability. A checklist for corrective action and corrective action don'ts will help guide you through the corrective action maze and help you make all the right decisions.

Chapter 7: "Building an Olympic Team and Going for the Gold"— Sexual Harassment Training. Developing a sexual harassment prevention policy and mastering the complaint, investigation, and corrective action process is only part of the battle against sexual harassment. Another critical need is to implement a comprehensive sexual harassment training program for all employees, from the mailroom clerk to the chief executive officer. Fighting sexual harassment and being aware of inappropriate behavior takes a combined team effort between management and the rank and file. All employees must be required to deal head-on with their behaviors on the job and make a commitment to be part of the team effort.

Chapter 7 explains how to design an effective training program tailored to the specific needs of your company and how to assess those needs. You will learn about the use of focus groups and how to choose the best format and methodology for your training program. A review of all the topics that must be addressed during the training, and a complete sample training outline are provided to help you spread the word about sexual harassment to the entire workforce.

Acknowledgments

Writing an easy-to-read book for managers about sexual harassment was quite an undertaking because sexual harassment is perhaps the most complex and delicate workplace discrimination issue there is today. To really convey in an uncomplicated way what every manager needs to know about it took a lot more than cracking a few law books or reading some court cases. This was one of those areas where we had to reach deep into our grab bag of experience in dealing with workplace issues from both a legal and a business perspective.

In order to offer detailed advice on how to handle sexual harassment issues, including how to recognize and change inappropriate behaviors, we drew on many of the actual complaints and court cases in which we had been called upon to defend or offer guidance. We also drew on the numerous seminars and training sessions that we have given over the years to a multitude of business clients. The issues raised in litigation and the questions asked by participants at our training sessions were the impetus for many of the management techniques and suggestions offered in this book.

Consequently, this book has many contributors. From the corporate giants to the "mom and pop" small businesses that have retained us, heard our warnings firsthand, and actually taken our advice, we salute you. We thank the manager who told us about his inappropriate sexual advances toward a subordinate. We thank the supervisor who shared her fears about observing rampant sexual misconduct on the shop floor. We thank the chief executive officer who so honestly disclosed his biases and stereotypical attitudes toward women. Without the candid observations and real-world experiences offered by our clients and their employees, we would never have been able to write this book, and we thank all of them for giving us the opportunity to share what we have learned for the benefit of others.

What Every Manager
Needs to Know About
Sexual Harassment

CHAPTER I

"I Know It When I See It"
The Meaning of Sexual Harassment

Recognizing sexual harassment is often no easy task because the workplace consists of many complicated interpersonal relationships and corporate structures or mentalities that may dictate how employees are expected to react toward one another. We all know that managers have different styles, personalities, and opinions, and they can be perceived in many ways. You may treat some subordinates favorably, while others get the cold shoulder, for a variety of reasons. You also may have a social relationship outside the office with some of your subordinates or co-managers, which will obviously affect how you treat these individuals on the job.

Relationships between coworkers also cover a wide spectrum, from the best of friends to archenemies. As a manager, you need to be perceptive about these relationships in order to assess any workplace misconduct, including sexual harassment. The scorned lover or the new office romance will have some bearing on how you interpret the conduct of your employees and decide whether certain conduct is merely inappropriate or offensive, with no legal consequences, or something more serious, which could put you and your company in legal jeopardy.

Sexual harassment is perhaps the most difficult type of employment discrimination to decipher and deal with because it is rooted in behaviors that strike at the most intimate, and perhaps confusing, aspect of human existence: a person's sexuality. Certainly, if you witness someone coming on to a coworker in a sexual way or grop-ing the mailroom clerk, you will probably conclude that such con-duct is likely to be sexual harassment and illegal. But what about more subtle conduct with sexual overtones? Perhaps all the press about sexual harassment in the past few years has forced alleged perpetrators to act in less direct, yet equally offensive ways. Conse-quently, even sophisticated and knowledgeable managers may have trouble recognizing sexual harassment.

Obviously, all managers must be able to identify sexual harass-ment and be familiar with the legal implications in order to deal with it effectively. Knowing the terminology and how the courts and agencies handle sexual harassment is a must. Also, knowing the behavioral warning signs and how to spot a possible offender can help you avoid sexual harassment complaints in the first place. If you learn nothing else from this chapter, you will learn to err on the side of safety. In other words, as a manager, you need to take a con-servative approach to sexual harassment. Even conduct appearing innocuous may be illegal, and every report, observation, or even office gossip should be taken seriously and investigated.

The theme throughout this chapter, and the entire book, is zero tolerance when it comes to sexual harassment. You, as a manager, along with all other company officials, need to stress this point whenever discussing the topic with your workforce. And remember that you need to monitor your own conduct to set an appropriate example with subordinates and to leave absolutely no impression that you are callous toward or uninterested in preventing and han-dling any sexually harassing conduct. It is essential to keep in mind that even if you personally do not find certain conduct to be sexually offensive, others might and often will.

Test Your Knowledge

What do you already know about sexual harassment? Do you think you can identify sexually harassing conduct? Can you distinguish between illegal sexual harassment and merely offensive conduct, which may not be illegal? Before reading this chapter, test your cur-rent knowledge. Following is a true-or-false test. The answers, with explanations, appear at the end of the chapter. Take the test now, putting a T (for true) or F (for false) next to each statement, and then take it again after you have read through and digested the information that follows. You may be surprised at the different results.

True or False?

_____ 1. If someone doesn't complain about being sexually harassed and you, as the manager, don't know about it, your company cannot be held legally responsible.

_____ 2. A manager cannot be held personally liable or have to pay damages for proved sexual harassment. Only the company can be held legally liable.

_____ 3. In order to win a sexual harassment case alleging a sexually hostile work environment, an employee has to prove that some adverse employment action was taken against him or her (e.g., discharge, demotion, pay cut).

_____ 4. If someone participates in sexually offensive behavior, the person cannot claim that he or she was sexually harassed.

_____ 5. A company can be liable for sexual harassment only when a manager or company official engages in sexually offensive conduct toward a subordinate.

_____ 6. It is illegal for a company not to have a written sexual harassment policy with a complaint procedure.

_____ 7. A man cannot sexually harass another man, nor can a woman sexually harass another woman.

_____ 8. A sexual harassment policy must state that employees are to report any sexually harassing conduct first to their immediate supervisor.

_____ 9. It is sexual harassment if a manager says to a subordinate, "Wow, you really look sexy today!"

10. The following conduct by a manager will always be considered sexual harassment:

_____ a. Lydia, a supervisor in an auto body shop, uses sexual terms and four-letter words to express herself whenever speaking to mechanics in the shop.

_____ b. Gerard, a sales manager, often tells sexual jokes to his subordinates.

_____ c. Denise, a vice president of an accounting firm, always gives her secretary the once-over with sexually suggestive eye contact.

_____ d. Sharon, a bank manager, keeps asking Marty, the receptionist, out for a date and drinks after work, telling him he needs "a real woman."

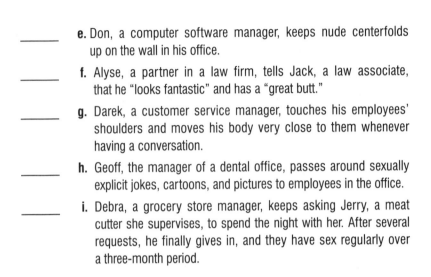

_____ **e.** Don, a computer software manager, keeps nude centerfolds up on the wall in his office.

_____ **f.** Alyse, a partner in a law firm, tells Jack, a law associate, that he "looks fantastic" and has a "great butt."

_____ **g.** Darek, a customer service manager, touches his employees' shoulders and moves his body very close to them whenever having a conversation.

_____ **h.** Geoff, the manager of a dental office, passes around sexually explicit jokes, cartoons, and pictures to employees in the office.

_____ **i.** Debra, a grocery store manager, keeps asking Jerry, a meat cutter she supervises, to spend the night with her. After several requests, he finally gives in, and they have sex regularly over a three-month period.

How Did It Come to This? A Short History of the Origins of Sexual Harassment

Most managers know that sex and other forms of discrimination in the workplace have been prohibited since Congress passed Title VII of the Civil Rights Act of 1964.[1] Title VII states that "it shall be an unlawful employment practice for an employer . . . to fail or refuse to hire or to discharge any individual, or otherwise to discriminate against any individual with respect to his compensation, terms, conditions, or privileges of employment, because of such individual's race, color, religion, sex, or national origin."[2]

For many years after passage of Title VII, the typical sex discrimination case usually involved a female applicant or employee who alleged that she was denied a job or was terminated because she was a woman. These cases often turned on evidence that few, if any, women had been considered for the job in question, or that male employees with less experience or qualifications were treated more favorably. However, as more women entered the workforce throughout the 1970s and early 1980s, a new breed of sex discrimination claim under Title VII, referred to as *sexual harassment*, began to take hold.

In the early days, a sexual harassment lawsuit usually involved a female employee asked by her boss to engage in sex, and if she refused, she was fired. Other individuals claimed that although there was no threat of or actual job loss, they were still being treated in an undignified and abusive manner because of their sex, including uninvited sexual comments, jokes, touching, and other inappropriate or degrading behavior of a sexual nature.

As these types of sex discrimination claims became more common, the U.S. Equal Employment Opportunity Commission (EEOC), the federal agency charged with administering Title VII, was prompted to issue guidelines on sexual harassment in 1980. These guidelines, while not binding on the federal courts, are still used by the courts today to help analyze sexual harassment complaints.

A "Defining Moment": The EEOC Tackles Sexual Harassment

The EEOC's guidelines recognized sexual harassment as a form of sex discrimination protected by Title VII and attempted to define the types of behaviors that were illegal. In a nutshell, the regulations define sexual harassment as follows:

> Unwelcome sexual advances, requests for sexual favors, and other verbal or physical conduct of a sexual nature constitutes sexual harassment when:
>
> 1. Submission to such conduct is made either explicitly or implicitly a term or condition of an individual's employment;
>
> 2. Submission to or rejection of such conduct by an individual is used as the basis for employment decisions affecting such individual; or
>
> 3. Such conduct has the purpose or effect of unreasonably interfering with an individual's work performance or creating an intimidating, hostile, or offensive working environment.[3]

The EEOC's definition of sexual harassment may appear to be short, but it is far from simple. Nearly twenty years have passed and the courts are still struggling to come up with understandable standards and clear definitions to assist companies and managers in dealing with sexual harassment complaints. However, the guidelines are helpful as a starting point to identify the two basic types of sexual harassment and to understand the parameters of what actually constitutes illegal behavior.

Unwanted, Uninvited, Unsolicited, and Unencouraged All Equal "Unwelcome"

In defining sexual harassment, the EEOC's guidelines state that a sexual advance, request for sexual favors, or sexually verbal or physical conduct must be "unwelcome." In other words, the complaining individual must show that he or she did not want, invite, solicit, or encourage the sexual conduct in order to show that sexual harassment actually occurred. A truly consensual sexual relationship or sexual conduct in which the alleged victim willingly participated or set in motion may not be considered unwelcome and hence, not sexual harassment.

For example, Dorothy is a real estate agent working in an office with several other agents. She constantly tells dirty jokes, makes obscene sexual gestures, and comes on to her coworkers with sexually suggestive comments. Other real estate agents in the office, both male and female, engage in similar conduct and respond to Dorothy's lewd and sexually oriented behavior. Dorothy later gets fired for performance reasons, and she sues the company for sexual harassment. Is the company off the hook? The answer is a cautious yes. If the company can show that Dorothy instigated the sexually offensive conduct or participated in and encouraged it when it was directed to her by other employees, it may be able to show that the sexually offensive conduct was not unwelcome by Dorothy, and consequently, no sexual harassment took place.

This example does not suggest that managers or coworkers should participate in conduct on the job that has sexual overtones simply because someone else may have started the ball rolling and it can be later argued that the conduct was not unwelcome. For many reasons, which will become abundantly clear as you read this book, a manager or a coworker who participates in or encourages any type of sexual behavior that could be considered inappropriate is acting at his or her own peril. If you have to ask yourself, "Could my behavior be sexually offensive to anyone," the answer is probably yes. The point is that although the sexual conduct at issue must be unwelcome in order to establish sexual harassment, that threshold issue is very hard to prove and should not be relied on with any great enthusiasm as a defense to a sexual harassment complaint, except in the clearest of circumstances.

Additionally, when the courts and the EEOC consider whether sexual conduct was unwelcome, they look at all the circumstances and concentrate on the alleged victim, not the alleged offender's intent. The fact that an alleged offender did not intend for his or her actions to be perceived as sexually offensive has no bearing whatsoever. The alleged victim's perception and the sexual actions that occurred are the only factors considered. More important, it is not necessary for the alleged victim to say, "Please stop. Your behavior is sexually offensive and unwelcomed by me." If the employee did complain, it strengthens her case that the conduct was unwelcome. However, in many cases, the alleged victim of sexual harassment says absolutely nothing, taking the sexually offensive conduct in stride for fear of being fired or suffering some other adverse employment consequence. Consequently, the best course is to assume that *any* sexual conduct is taboo at the workplace, whether or not it may legally be construed as sexual harassment.

"This for That" or Quid Pro Quo Sexual Harassment

Keeping in mind that any type of sexual harassment has to be unwelcome, the first two definitions of sexual harassment under the EEOC's guidelines are commonly referred to as *quid pro quo sexual harassment*. This is usually the most direct and obvious type of sexual harassment. It typically occurs when some job penalty or benefit (e.g., a term or condition of employment) is given, based on the individual's acceptance or rejection of a request for sexual favors. A "term or condition of employment" is broadly construed and is not confined to job security alone. In other words, a request for sexual favors can be conditioned on changes in compensation, job transfers, promotions, work schedules, bonuses, and just about any other matter that affects an individual's employment.

An example of quid pro quo sexual harassment would be a manager asking his secretary to go to bed with him and telling her that if she refuses, she'll be fired, or if she accepts, she'll be promoted. When she does in fact refuse, she is terminated. When and if she accepts, she does get the promotion.

Recent U.S. Supreme Court decisions require that there must be a tangible effect on the terms or conditions of an individual's employment based on an unwelcome sexual advance in order to find quid pro quo sexual harassment.[4] These cases also instruct that liability for quid pro quo sexual harassment is absolute. In other words, barring proof that the conduct was not "unwelcome," there are no defenses.

This scenario clearly fits part 2 of the EEOC's definition of sexual harassment, stating that if acceptance or rejection of a sexual proposition is in fact used as the basis for an employment decision, then there is absolutely no question that quid pro quo sexual harassment has occurred. Thus, when the boss tells his secretary to clean out her desk the day after she rejects his request to sleep with him, it is fairly easy to prove that the discharge was prompted by the secretary's rejection of his sexual proposition. It also fits the EEOC's statement in part 1 of the guidelines that "submission to such conduct is made . . . explicitly a term or condition of an individual's employment."

However, part 1 of the EEOC's definition of sexual harassment also states that submission can implicitly be made a term or condition of employment. This involves more subtle requests for sexual favors where the meaning of the statement is clearly implied. Some of these more subtle, or implicit, threats and promises include the following statements made by managers:

> "I'd love it if you would take that business trip with me, and we can share a room. When we get back, I'll see what I can do about that promotion you want."

> "You know, if you acted a little friendlier, I might be able to get you a raise."

> "I don't know if I can recommend you for that job transfer because I feel as if I don't really know you well enough. Maybe if we went to dinner and got closer, I'd be able to help you out."

> "Wearing shorter skirts may help you get that part-time schedule you've been wanting."

> "Your bonus could be a lot bigger next time if you'd just have that drink with me after work."

"You might want to consider going out with me if you really want that bigger office."

The meaning of these statements is clear. If the individual "shares that room" or "has that drink after work," a job penalty or benefit will be given. More important, if the job penalty or benefit is actually carried out, quid pro quo sexual harassment will be found.

This does not mean that a threat or promise conditioned on a sexual favor that is not carried out will be ignored when it comes to establishing sexual harassment. Unfulfilled threats or promises will still be considered as evidence of "hostile environment" sexual harassment, the second type of sexual harassment discussed in detail below. The significance of this distinction is that in hostile environment cases, an employer may raise some affirmative defenses, whereas in the quid pro quo situation (e.g., the threat or promise materializes), there are no affirmative defenses.

The bottom line is that no manager should ever, even jokingly, make a statement that could be interpreted as some type of sexual proposition in exchange for a job benefit or penalty. Liability for such remarks can be absolute. Your company can be held responsible for sexual harassment, and your job security will surely be on the line.

"I Can't Take It Anymore," or Hostile-Environment Sexual Harassment

Part 3 of the EEOC's guidelines identifies what has become known as "hostile-environment sexual harassment." In its most basic form, hostile-environment sexual harassment usually involves a situation where the workplace is replete with sexual comments, innuendos, jokes, inappropriate touching, or other degrading or abusive conduct of a sexual nature that is repeated and continuous over a period of time, becoming so bad that the average or "reasonable" person finds it intolerable. Such conduct is viewed as having the purpose or effect of unreasonably interfering with an individual's work performance based on the individual's sex and, hence, a violation of Title VII. There does not have to be an actual or threatened job perk or penalty for an individual to establish that he or she was subjected to a sexually hostile working environment.

Managers need to be familiar with two buzzwords used by the EEOC and the courts to identify hostile-environment sexual harassment: *severe* and *pervasive*. This generally means that the sexual conduct must be extreme and repeated and continuous in order to rise to the level of a hostile environment. It usually needs to be something more than an offhand sexual comment or a lewd sexual joke. In other words, not all sexually offensive conduct is illegal sexual harassment. For example, an isolated remark by a manager about his subordinate's breasts may be totally inappropriate, but would not constitute sexual harassment because it would not be severe or pervasive enough to create a hostile environment using a "reasonable person" standard. Similarly, mere discourtesy, rudeness, teasing, sexual jokes, offhand sexual comments, or a lack of sensitivity toward someone because of his or her sex may not amount to unlawful sexual harassment if such conduct is not repeated or continuous, or if the incident is not conduct of a sexual nature. Calling someone an adulterer or home wrecker, for instance, may have some remote sexual connotation, but it would most likely not be viewed as sexual harassment. Also, keep in mind that the general requirement that sexually offensive conduct must be repeated or continuous may have no bearing if sexual physical contact is involved. For example, touching someone's breast or other sexual body part, even if done just one time, may be enough to establish hostile-environment sexual harassment. Again, hostile-environment sexual harassment depends on the severity of the conduct. It must be extreme.

Both objective and subjective factors must be assessed when trying to determine whether there is a hostile environment. Objectively, at a minimum you need to consider (1) the frequency of the conduct; (2) its severity; (3) whether it is physically threatening or humiliating, or merely an isolated offensive incident; and (4) whether the sexual conduct interferes with the complaining employee's work performance. Subjectively, you need to consider whether the complaining employee perceived the conduct to be sexually hostile or abusive.

Hostile-environment sexual harassment is sometimes difficult to identify because the offensive acts are not always clearly sexual in nature. For example, constantly poking fun at women based on stereotypes that are not technically sexual or repeatedly excluding men from certain activities simply because they are men could still constitute sexual harassment in some cases because the offensive conduct is based on the person's gender. Such conduct aimed at a person because of his or her sex can constitute a hostile or abusive working environment, which is presumed to adversely affect the individual's job and productivity.

Trying to wade through all the factors that can amount to hostile environment sexual harassment is a dangerous game for managers to play. The factors cannot always be easily identified or interpreted. So why not play it safe? If you observe sexual conduct that even remotely appears to be offensive, you should stop it, and stop it fast.

Finally, the defenses to a hostile-environment claim are limited at best in light of recent U.S. Supreme Court decisions, which are discussed in more detail later in this chapter. Simply having a sexual harassment policy in place and taking prompt corrective action when confronted with a hostile environment complaint may not get you off the hook. The courts are taking a much harder stance against sexual harassment, and although you may have some defenses to hostile-environment claims, your odds of winning a case will often be slim.

If You Have to Ask, It Probably Is: Examples of Inappropriate Behavior

Because hostile-environment sexual harassment is sometimes hard to pinpoint, it is helpful to review some of the conduct that can constitute the offense and has been recognized in various court cases as amounting to hostile-environment sexual harassment. Most of the court cases and legal wrangling center around this type of sexual harassment because it is harder to identify and usually does not involve a tangible job benefit or penalty. As you review the examples of sexually offensive conduct, remember that the conduct must be severe and pervasive, meaning that it generally has to be repeated or continuous, and intolerable based on a "reasonable person" standard. Generally, if you find yourself asking whether certain conduct of a sexual nature could be evidence of sexual harassment, the answer is probably yes. The following examples are by no means inclusive, but many of them have been deemed evidence of hostile-environment sexual harassment:

- Explicit sexual propositions or pressuring someone for a date or sex

- Touching or other persistent sexual advances

- Sexual innuendos, stories, jokes, or suggestive comments

- Sexually oriented "kidding" or "teasing"

- Practical jokes of a sexual nature

- Jokes about gender-specific traits or denigrating gender-specific remarks

- Sexually oriented letters, telephone calls, e-mails, or faxes

- Turning work discussions into sexual topics

- Bragging about sexual prowess

- Asking personal questions about a coworker's social or sex life

- Giving compliments with sexual overtones

- Making sexual comments about an individual's clothing, body, or looks

- Telling lies or spreading rumors about a coworker's sex life

- Touching a coworker's clothing, hair, or body or giving a neck massage

- Referring to someone as a *doll, babe, honey, hunk, beefcake,* or similar other term

- Hanging around a coworker when there is no business reason

- Hugging, kissing, patting, pinching, brushing against, or stroking a coworker

- Staring at a coworker's body parts or engaging in sexually suggestive eye contact during conversations

- Coming very close to someone when speaking (e.g., always leaning over or cornering someone) or using a suggestive voice

- Passing around or displaying sexually suggestive or foul visual materials (e.g., pinups, cartoons) or downloading sexual material or pictures on the computer

- Using foul or obscene language or gestures (e.g., whistling, catcalls)

Must Reading: U.S. Supreme Court Cases

Until the mid-1980s, the U.S. Supreme Court seemed to ignore sexual harassment cases, refusing to consider hundreds of appeals from the lower federal courts. This sometimes resulted in inconsistent, poorly reasoned lower court decisions that gave managers, and employers in general, limited guidance on how to identify and handle sexual harassment complaints. It was not until 1986 that the Supreme Court affirmed the existence of quid pro quo claims and for the first time recognized that hostile-environment sexual harassment was also a form of sex discrimination prohibited by Title VII. In the landmark case of *Meritor Savings Bank v. Vinson*, the Court stated that "a plaintiff may establish a violation of Title VII by proving that discrimination based on sex has created a hostile or abusive work environment."[5]

Mechelle Vinson's Sexual Encounters

Background

Mechelle Vinson was hired in 1974 as a bank teller trainee by Sidney Taylor, a vice president of Meritor Savings Bank. She worked at the bank for over four years and received several promotions from Taylor, who was her supervisor during the entire time of her employment. Shortly after Vinson notified the bank in 1978 that she needed an indefinite period of time off for sick leave, she was fired. Subsequently, she sued both Taylor and the bank, claiming that throughout her employment, she had constantly been subjected to sexual harassment by Taylor.

Vinson claimed that when she was first promoted, Taylor asked her to dinner and she accepted. During the course of the meal, he suggested that they go to a motel to have sex. Although Vinson said she initially refused, she eventually gave in because she feared she would lose her job. Taylor's demands for sex did not stop after the first encounter. According to Vinson, Taylor made repeated demands in the months and years that followed, both during and after business hours. Vinson claimed that she continued to have sex with him and estimated that she had engaged in intercourse with Taylor some forty or fifty times.

She also alleged that Taylor had fondled her in front of other employees, followed her into the women's rest room, exposed himself to her, forcibly raped her on several occasions, and had touched and fondled other female employees. Vinson said that she never reported Taylor's "harassment" to any bank managers and that she never attempted to use the bank's complaint procedure because she was afraid of Taylor.

Not surprisingly, Taylor denied all the allegations and even asserted that he never had sexual relations with Vinson. Instead, he claimed that Vinson was making her accusations because she had been fired. Both Taylor and the bank argued that the sexual encounters, if they occurred at all, were voluntary on Vinson's part, based, in part, on evidence that she wore provocative clothing and discussed her personal fantasies with Taylor and other employees. The bank also denied any wrongdoing, claiming that even if Vinson's allegations were true, it had no knowledge of any sexual harassment, it never gave its approval or consent to Taylor's alleged actions, and Vinson never used the bank's internal complaint procedure for resolving discrimination claims.

The Rulings

A federal trial court ruled that Vinson was not the victim of sexual harassment, stating that if a sexual relationship had occurred, it was voluntary and had nothing to do with Vinson's continued employment at the bank or her promotions. Vinson appealed that ruling, and the appeals court ruled that further proceedings were necessary to determine if Vinson had actually been subjected to hostile-environment sexual harassment.

The Supreme Court agreed that there could be liability on the part of Taylor and the bank if Vinson's claims were proved. First, the Court recognized that without question, when a supervisor sexually harasses a subordinate because of the subordinate's sex, that supervisor discriminates on the basis of sex, and a violation of Title VII will be found. It then stated, however, that sexual harassment claims do not have to be premised on "tangible" or "economic" losses in the workplace (e.g., discharge, demotion) and that simply subjecting an individual to a "hostile or abusive work environment" because of that individual's sex would suffice to alter the individual's terms or conditions of employment, and amount to sexual harassment in violation of Title VII. Hostile-environment sexual harassment was now formally recognized as an alternative type of sexual harassment for which damages could be recovered.

The Supreme Court cautioned that hostile-environment sexual harassment had to be sufficiently "severe and pervasive" to be valid. Otherwise, it would not be viewed as having altered the victim's terms or conditions of employment to a degree of sex discrimination that would be protected by Title VII. Vinson's claims, on the other hand, if proved, were viewed by the Supreme Court to be sufficiently severe and pervasive to establish a claim for hostile-environment sexual harassment. It sent her case back to the trial court for further proceedings.

The Supreme Court also discussed whether Taylor's sexual advances were "unwelcomed" by Vinson. In that regard, it looked at whether Vinson voluntarily had sex with Taylor and whether that could be a defense to her sexual harassment claim. Without much elaboration, the Supreme Court stated that Vinson could have voluntarily engaged in sex, in the sense that she was not forced to participate against her will, yet still show that Taylor's sexual advances were unwelcomed by her. The Court even ruled that evidence of Vinson's sexually provocative dress and speech were relevant factors to consider in determining whether Taylor's sexual propositions were unwelcome.

Finally, the Supreme Court addressed the bank's defenses to the lawsuit. Could the bank be held liable for sexual harassment when it had no knowledge of Taylor's conduct? Vinson admittedly failed to report the alleged incidents and failed to use the bank's internal grievance procedure for discrimination claims. Here, the Court fell short of making a definitive ruling, saying only that an employer will not always be absolutely liable for the acts of its supervisors in hostile-environment cases, but the fact that the employer had no notice about a supervisor's sexual harassment will not necessarily prevent liability.

Furthermore, the mere fact that a grievance procedure was in effect but not used by Vinson was not a complete defense for the bank because it was only a general nondiscrimination policy that did not specifically address sexual harassment or encourage employees to come forth with such claims. It also required an employee to complain first to her supervisor. In the Court's view, because Taylor was the supervisor, as well as the alleged perpetrator, it was not surprising that Vinson chose not to use the procedure and report her complaint to him.

After Mechelle Vinson's case, the Supreme Court made no significant rulings about sexual harassment until 1993, when Teresa Harris, a manager of an equipment rental company, sued her employer for hostile environment sexual harassment.

Teresa Harris's Lack of "Injury"

Background

In *Harris v. Forklift Systems, Inc.,* Teresa Harris worked for the company for about two years.[6] During that time, Charles Hardy, the company's president, often insulted her and made her the target of sexual jokes and innuendos. On several occasions, in the presence of coworkers, Hardy said to Harris, "You're a woman, what do you know?" and, "We need a man as the rental manager." Hardy even called Harris "a dumb ass woman."

On other occasions, again in front of other employees, Hardy told Harris that the two of them should "go to the Holiday Inn to negotiate [Harris's] raise." He asked Harris and other female employees to get coins from his front pants pocket. He also threw objects on the ground and asked Harris and other female employees to pick them up while he watched. Finally, Hardy made several remarks to Harris of a sexual nature about her clothing and the clothes worn by other female employees.

After several months of these incidents, Harris finally complained directly to Hardy about his conduct. Hardy said he was surprised that Harris was offended, claimed that he was only joking, and apologized. When he also promised to stop, Harris decided to stay on the job because of his assurances. However, less than one month later, Hardy's comments started again. On one occasion while Harris was working on a deal with a customer, Hardy said, in front of other employees, "What did you do, promise the guy . . . some [sex] Saturday night?" Shortly after, Teresa Harris quit her job and sued the company for sexual harassment.

The Rulings

Although a federal trial court found that the evidence amounted to a "close case," it ruled that Teresa Harris had not been subjected to hostile-environment sexual harassment because even though the company president's conduct was offensive, it was not so severe as "to seriously affect Harris's psychological well-being." The trial court thus believed that in order to win her case, Harris had to show that the sexually harassing conduct caused her to suffer a serious effect on her "psychological well-being" or some other tangible injury.

The Supreme Court disagreed. It held that a sexually abusive work environment, even one that does not seriously affect an employee's psychological well-being, can and often will detract from an employee's job performance, discourage her from remaining on the job, or keep her from advancing in her career. In other words, to prove hostile-environment sexual harassment, an employee does not have to show that she suffered any concrete psychological harm or other injury, but only that the environment would be perceived by a "reasonable person" to be sexually hostile or abusive.

The Supreme Court also confirmed that both objective and subjective factors had to be considered to determine whether there was in fact a hostile or abusive working environment, including the frequency of the discriminatory conduct; its severity; whether it is physically threatening or humiliating, or merely an offensive utterance; and whether it unreasonably interferes with an employee's work performance. On the subjective side, the inquiry is whether the complaining employee would perceive the environment to be sexually hostile or abusive. On this point, the Court agreed that the effect on the employee's psychological well-being would be one factor to look at when trying to determine whether she actually found the conduct to be abusive.

Teresa Harris's case established that in order to have a viable claim for hostile environment sexual harassment, there must be objective evidence of extreme sexually offensive conduct and subjective evidence that the alleged victim perceived the conduct to be offensive using a "reasonable person" standard. Moreover, the alleged victim does not have to suffer psychological or other tangible injuries.

Are There Any Defenses to a Sexual Harassment Claim?

Defenses to a sexual harassment claim are limited; in the case of quid pro quo sexual harassment, they are virtually nonexistent. Nevertheless, in both quid pro quo and hostile-environment cases, the first line of defense is that the conduct complained of was not unwelcome by the complaining employee. Thus, if you or another manager are foolish enough to ask a subordinate to sleep with you, and you can establish that he or she made or encouraged the sexual proposition, you may be off the hook. But this is no easy task. The courts, and particularly a jury, will look at your actions with a magnifying glass and perhaps lean toward the subordinate in a he said/she said battle. Similarly, in the hostile-environment context, you would need to show that the complaining employee prompted, participated in, or invited the sexual behavior at issue. Again, raising the "unwelcome" defense in these circumstances will be no piece of cake, considering that such determinations are based on subjective standards. How can you assess what the complaining employee was really thinking, despite his or her own questionable conduct? After the "unwelcome" defense is exhausted, the choices are limited, and they depend on the type of sexual harassment at issue.

The EEOC's guidelines, while not binding on the federal courts, shed some light on how responsibility for sexual harassment is viewed:

> [An employer] is responsible for the acts and those of its agents and supervisory employees with respect to sexual harassment regardless of whether the specific acts complained of were authorized or even forbidden by the employer and regardless of whether the employer knew or should have known of their occurrence.[7]

In other words, a manager's sexually harassing behavior subjects his or her employer to liability even if there is a policy forbidding such conduct and even if upper management had no clue as to what was going on.

The EEOC's guidelines are most relevant in quid pro quo cases. There is always "strict liability" in those situations, meaning that the employer is completely and absolutely responsible for any harm caused to an employee because of a manager's sexually harassing conduct. There is simply no defense to a proven quid pro quo claim. The rationale behind this kind of liability is that a supervisor or manager is the agent of the company and is presumed to act with the company's blessing.

In hostile-environment sexual harassment cases, an employer's liability for the conduct of its managers is not absolute, although the defenses are limited. First, an employer can always argue that the conduct complained of was not "severe and pervasive" or extreme enough to amount to a hostile environment. However, if the facts are such that a hostile environment is clearly present, an employer has few choices, as illustrated by two recent U.S. Supreme Court cases.

The Supreme Court basically remained silent on sexual harassment for several years after the *Vinson* and *Harris* decisions, but in 1998, it finally spoke again in two landmark cases decided on the same day, *Burlington Industries v. Ellerth* and *Faragher v. City of Boca Raton.*[8] These recent cases reaffirmed many principles of the earlier Supreme Court decisions and substantially altered the law concerning an employer's defenses for the sexually harassing conduct of its supervisors or managers.

Kimberly Ellerth's Obnoxious Manager

Kimberly Ellerth worked as a salesperson in the Chicago office of Burlington Industries. Over the course of her employment she was repeatedly propositioned and harassed by a "midlevel manager," Ted Slowik, who was located in New York and had supervisory responsibility for the Chicago office, but he was not Ellerth's immediate supervisor. On one occasion while on a business trip, Slowik propositioned Ellerth for sex in a hotel cocktail lounge, and when she said no, he made remarks about her breasts and told her to "loosen up." He then warned, "You know, Kim, I could make your life very hard or very easy at Burlington."

On another occasion, Slowik threatened to hold up a promotion for Ellerth, telling her she was not "loose enough," and rubbing her knee during the promotion interview. She did get the promotion, but when Slowik called to give the news, he said, "You're gonna be out there with men who work in factories, and they certainly like women with pretty butts and legs." Two months later, Ellerth called Slowik to ask about a fabric sample, and Slowik responded, "I don't have time for you right now, Kim, unless you want to tell me what you're wearing." During another telephone call a few days later, Slowik asked, "Are you wearing shorter skirts yet, Kim? Because it would make your job a whole heck of a lot easier."

Despite all these incidents, Slowik's "threats" to Ellerth about her job security were never carried out, even though she rejected his sexual advances. However, a short time later, when Ellerth was cautioned by her immediate supervisor to return customer calls more promptly, she quit. At first, she did not say that she quit because of sexual harassment, but later she sent a letter to the company explaining that she had quit because of Slowik's behavior. Ellerth had never informed anyone in authority at the company, prior to her post-termination letter, about Slowik's conduct, even though she knew that the company had a written policy and procedure against sexual harassment.

The case went to the Supreme Court on the question of whether a claim of quid pro quo sexual harassment can be stated under Title VII where the harassed employee has not submitted to the sexual overtures of her boss and has not suffered any adverse employment action because of those refusals. Stated another way, the question presented was whether the "unfulfilled threats" of a manager whose sexual advances have been rebuffed are still sufficient to hold the employer responsible under Title VII.

Beth Ann Faragher's "Fun" in the Sun

Beth Ann Faragher worked for five summers as an ocean lifeguard for the Parks and Recreation Department of the City of Boca Raton, Florida. During those summers, two of Faragher's male lifeguard supervisors, Bill Terry and David Silverman, regularly propositioned her for sex, offensively touched her, made demeaning, lewd, and offensive sexual comments about her and women in general, and sexually harassed other female lifeguards.

Terry stated that he would never promote a woman, repeatedly touched the bodies of female lifeguards without invitation, put his arm around Faragher and one hand on her buttock, grabbed another female lifeguard in a "sexual simulation" motion, made a disparaging comment about Faragher's shape, and asked another female lifeguard during an interview if she would have sex with male lifeguards because that often occurred.

Silverman's conduct was equally offensive. He once said to Faragher, "Date me or clean the toilets for a year." He once tackled Faragher, remarking that if it wasn't for a certain physical characteristic of hers, he would readily have sex with her. Another time he pantomimed an act of oral sex. Silverman also made frequent vulgar references to women and sexual matters, commented on the bodies of female lifeguards and beach-goers, and at least twice told female lifeguards that he would like to engage in sex with them.

Faragher never complained to higher management about her supervisors' conduct. During the trial, it also came out that the city had a written sexual harassment policy but had failed to distribute the policy to the lifeguards or their supervisors. On the basis of another female lifeguard's complaints to the city, the city investigated and found that Terry and Silverman had indeed behaved improperly. They were reprimanded and given the choice between a suspension without pay or the forfeiture of annual leave.

The federal trial court concluded that the supervisors' conduct was sufficiently severe and pervasive to satisfy the standards for creating a sexually hostile work environment under Title VII. Nonetheless, because Faragher never complained to higher management, she was awarded only one dollar for her Title VII claim. She appealed. The court of appeals reversed the award, concluding that the city could not be held liable for its supervisors' sexual misconduct because it had never been notified of Faragher's claim. The issue before the Supreme Court was whether the city could still be liable for the unreported conduct of its supervisory staff.

The Supreme Court's Analysis: Clearer or Murkier Guidance for Managers?

In both *Ellerth* and *Faragher*, the Supreme Court attempted to "assist in defining the relevant standards of employer liability" for the sexually harassing misconduct of supervisors. Although both decisions were by a clear majority of the Court, with two dissenting justices, it is ultimately questionable as to whether the law has been made murkier or clearer by these decisions. Whatever that outcome, however, *Ellerth* and *Faragher* changed the law on liability for sexual harassment.

First, the Court stepped away from labeling sexual harassment as quid pro quo or "hostile environment" when trying to decide whether an employer is liable for the sexually harassing conduct of its managers. While not abandoning those terms entirely, the Court made clear that a quid pro quo claim exists only when an employee has suffered an adverse employment action (e.g., hiring, firing, failure to promote, significant change in responsibilities or benefits) because he or she failed to assent to a supervisor's sexual advances. In those cases, there are no affirmative defenses; the employer is always liable short of trying to prove that the sexual harassment was not "unwelcome."

In hostile-environment sexual harassment cases, employer liability is not as absolute. First, if threats are made but not carried out, as they were in Kimberly Ellerth's case, the sexual harassment is not quid pro quo, and an employer will have a chance to raise an affirmative defense to liability for a manager's sexually harassing behavior. Consequently, in both *Ellerth* and *Faragher*, the issue boiled down to determining the employer's liability in sexual harassment cases that proved to be a hostile work environment, but the victim was not subjected to any ultimate adverse employment consequences such as being terminated.

Turning to "general agency principles of law" (that an employer is generally responsible for the conduct of its supervisor/agents), the Court concluded that an employer is responsible for the sexually harassing conduct of its managers, subject to an opportunity to present an affirmative defense that has two components: (1) that the employer exercised reasonable care to prevent and promptly correct any sexually harassing behavior, and (2) that the employee unreasonably failed to take advantage of any preventive or corrective opportunities provided by the employer or to otherwise avoid harm.

The Court also commented on the circumstances under which the employer's defense may or may not succeed. First, when attempting to show that it reasonably tried to prevent and correct sexually harassing behavior, an employer without a sexual harassment policy and complaint procedure will be at a disadvantage. In other words, any employer without a comprehensive written sexual harassment policy, which includes an appropriate complaint procedure, is asking for trouble. Second, showing that the employee failed to use the complaint procedure will normally suffice to establish that the employee unreasonably failed to correct or avoid the sexually harassing behavior.

Applying this standard in *Ellerth*, the Court concluded that she should have the opportunity to prove that Slowik's actions were severe and pervasive enough to establish a hostile environment claim for which Burlington would be liable, subject to its ability to prove the affirmative defense. In *Faragher*, the Court summarily ruled against the employer, not giving it a chance to raise the affirmative defense because the facts already established that, as matter of law, the defense would fail since the city had not even distributed its sexual harassment policy to the workforce.

What Does It All Mean?

You have probably realized by now that the defenses to sexual harassment are fading fast. With the courts taking a harder line on employers, the best and perhaps the only real defense is prevention, for several reasons. First, if an adverse employment action has occurred, then there is essentially no defense at all. Second, if no adverse employment action has occurred, then once the employee has shown that there was a sexually hostile work environment by satisfying the "severe and pervasive" standard of conduct, liability will still be automatic unless the employer can prove the affirmative defense articulated by the Supreme Court in *Ellerth* and *Faragher*. Third, and perhaps most important, both elements of that affirmative defense must be present; in other words, the employer must have taken appropriate action to prevent and remedy the sexual harassment, and the employee must have failed to act reasonably to avoid it.

Prior to these recent Supreme Court cases, courts generally agreed that if an employer had a policy against sexual harassment and took prompt corrective action in a hostile-environment sexual harassment case, the employer was legally off the hook. Now, even if an employer has an effective sexual harassment policy in place that has been distributed to its employees, and it took prompt remedial action to correct the problem, it will still be held liable for supervisory sexual misconduct so long as the employee acted reasonably to protect himself or herself by reporting the misconduct and following the procedures.

In those cases, the employer will be limited to reducing the employee's damages claim because of the prompt remedial action it took, but it will not avoid liability altogether. The bottom line is that even when the employer has acted reasonably, liability may become the rule rather than the exception in most sexual harassment cases because the employer's defense options have been stripped to the bone.

Only in the clearest cases—the employer has a well-publicized and clearly written sexual harassment policy that the victim totally ignores—is the employer likely to prevail as a matter of law, and even then the "reasonableness" of the employee's failure to use the available complaint procedures could be an issue for trial. Employers who do not have a written policy in place that makes it easy for employees to seek redress for their claims, or who do not regularly revisit those policies with their entire workforce, will have no defense available to them other than asserting that the complained-of conduct was not "severe and pervasive" enough to constitute sexual harassment in the first place. In this regard, an employer who takes immediate and effective action to stop sexual harassment may be able to persuade a court to consider that as one factor in support of the employer's defense that the conduct was not "severe and pervasive" because of the employer's prompt reaction.

Finally, *Ellerth* dealt with a "midlevel manager." The Supreme Court took special care to state that it was not dealing with a case in which the supervisor being accused of misconduct was at such a high-level management position (i.e., the president or CEO) that his or her "high rank in the company makes him or her the employer's alter ego." The implication is that in those cases, employer liability may be automatic without the possibility of an affirmative defense, and even though the employee claiming sexual harassment did not suffer any adverse job action. That issue is likely to be litigated and someday may be separately addressed by the Supreme Court. Employers for now would be wise to assume, however, that the higher up a manager is in the company, the more likely it is that strict liability will apply to his or her action, and thus it is especially important to police the conduct of higher management and demand and receive absolute compliance with the mandates of Title VII by those individuals.

Other Important Issues

Sexual harassment is not confined to a manager's sexually offensive conduct or only to members of the opposite sex. Employers can be held legally responsible for sexual harassment between coworkers or even when a customer or vendor sexually harasses one of its employees. As a manager in these situations, you have an obligation to report any possible sexual harassment to senior management. Otherwise, your company may be held responsible, and your job could be on the line.

Sexual Harassment Between Coworkers and by Nonemployees

The EEOC's guidelines on sexual harassment are a good starting point for understanding how that agency and the courts view sexual harassment between coworkers and by nonemployees, as well as a manager's responsibilities in that regard. The guidelines state that an employer and its agents (e.g., managers and supervisors) are responsible for sexual harassment between coworkers if they knew or should have known about the conduct, unless it can be shown that they took immediate and appropriate corrective action.[9]

Although the Supreme Court in *Ellerth* and *Faragher* limited an employer's defenses for sexual harassment by a manager or supervisor, those cases did not address the standards to be applied for determining liability when sexual harassment by coworkers is at issue. Thus, it is fairly safe to assume that the courts will continue to follow the EEOC's guidelines, which basically impose a "negligence" standard on employers. This means that managers who look the other way or fail to recognize the telltale signs of sexually harassing conduct will be considered negligent in that they knew or should have known that the conduct was occurring. They will also be deemed negligent if they recognize sexual harassment but fail to do anything about it. In both scenarios, the employer will be found liable for coworker sexual harassment.

Obviously, sexual harassment between coworkers arises only in the hostile work environment situation. It is not applicable to quid pro quo sexual harassment because there is no manager suggesting a job penalty or benefit conditioned on a sexual proposition. In the typical coworker sexual harassment case, employees may play practical jokes with sexual overtones, make lewd sexual comments or gestures, engage in sexual touching of coworkers, criticize, threaten, or degrade coworkers because of their sex or body type, and generally engage in sexually offensive conduct. When one of the employees complains, all the standards that apply to a manager's behavior for determining whether hostile-environment sexual harassment has occurred will be considered.

Was the conduct "severe and pervasive"? Was it repeated and continuous? Was it "unwelcome" by the complaining employee? Would a "reasonable person" find the conduct to be sexually hostile or abusive? All of these questions need to be asked, and a manager needs to act quickly. Any manager who adequately supervises his or her employees will recognize a potential sexual harassment situation. If the complaining employee establishes a sexually hostile work environment and the employer took no prompt action to end and correct the situation, legal liability will surely follow. Even if no one complains, a manager has an obligation to stop sexual harassment as soon as it arises, and stop it fast. You also have an obligation to discipline any offenders promptly. Immediate and appropriate corrective action is the key to insulating your company from liability for sexual harassment by or among coworkers.

Keep in mind, however, that you should never bypass or act independently of a company policy or procedure that requires you to report sexual harassment to your superiors before taking any action. Many companies prohibit first-line managers from taking corrective or disciplinary action directly. They are often required to report any incidents first to the human resources department or some other personnel function. Only after consideration by that entity will a decision be made on how to proceed. If your company has such a procedure, by all means follow it. Never take action against your subordinates without proper authority from senior management.

An employer also can be held responsible for sexual harassment perpetrated by a customer, client, vendor, or some other nonemployee. In this regard the EEOC's guidelines also state that the employer is responsible where it knew or should have known of the conduct and failed to take immediate and appropriate corrective action. However, the EEOC's guidelines and the courts recognize that an employer may not always have any control or legal responsibility over a customer or other nonemployee and when deciding liability, this factor will be considered.[10]

Some of the nonemployee sexual harassment cases involve employer dress codes, a customer or vendor asking an employee for sexual favors, or a perception by an employee that being receptive to sexual advances is "part of the job." For example, if a female employee is required to wear a skimpy cocktail waitress outfit or some other revealing attire and is subjected to catcalls, derogatory sexual comments, pinching, patting, and the like by customers, the employer can be held liable under the theory that requiring such attire would knowingly subject the employee to sexual harassment.[11]

Additionally, a direct request by a customer or vendor for sexual favors from an employee must be stopped as soon as you become aware of it. Even if the employee does not complain, employers are judged by the "knew or should have known" standard. This basically means that if you see such conduct or hear about it from other employees, you have an obligation to act immediately. With regard to taking immediate and appropriate corrective action when dealing with nonemployee sexual harassers, an employer may be limited in its options, but it can stop doing business with a particular vendor or tell a customer he or she is no longer welcome at the place of business.

Finally, managers in certain work environments, such as those catering to a "party crowd" (e.g., bars, restaurants, nightclubs, casinos), should take special care to avoid an employee's perceiving that a customer's sexual advance is acceptable or that the employee should be receptive to such behavior. The cocktail waitress is a good example. She may feel compelled to play along with a nonemployee sexual harasser because of management's casual attitude about sexual harassment or its subtle encouragement for employees to work the crowd for bigger tips and bar tabs. Remember that an employee's perception of management's attitude about sexual harassment, even if untrue, can set the tone at the workplace and increase the likelihood of a complaint being lodged.

Same-Sex Harassment

The Supreme Court ruled in *Oncale v. Sundowner Offshore Services, Inc.*, that sexual harassment can occur between two people of the same sex.[12] Joseph Oncale was a roustabout on an eight-man crew on an offshore oil platform in the Gulf of Mexico. After experiencing repeated sex-related harassment by his male coworkers and supervisors, including a physical assault and threat of rape, Oncale quit his job and sued for sex discrimination under Title VII. The lower courts threw his case out, ruling that no matter how offensive the conduct, Oncale had no right to sue under Title VII for harassment by his male coworkers. The Supreme Court unanimously reversed the lower court and concluded that "nothing in Title VII necessarily bars a claim of discrimination 'because of . . . sex' merely because the plaintiff and the defendant (or the person charged with acting on behalf of the defendant) are of the same sex."

The impact of *Oncale* is clear. An employer must protect against same-sex harassment just as it must protect against opposite-sex harassment. Harassing conduct need not be motivated by sexual desire in order to be actionable, and the standards in same-sex cases will be the same as in opposite-sex cases: whether the sex-based conduct is sufficiently severe and pervasive to create an objectively hostile or abusive work environment.

The Ten Most "Dangerous" Personality Types

As the courts continue to hammer out more definitive legal standards for dealing with sexual harassment while whittling away at an employer's defenses, it has become even more important to recognize a potential sexual harasser and to take action before a situation becomes serious.

Prevention is the key. No manager or company will survive the onslaught of sexual harassment claims without taking a proactive role. Sometimes people do not even realize that their behavior could be offensive, and a simple discussion may end the matter. Therefore, it is essential for every manager to watch the behaviors of coworkers, including other managers, and to report and deal with questionable conduct. When it comes to sexual harassment, recognizing the ten most dangerous personality types that follow is your first step toward prevention.

1. *The dirty jokester/office clown.* Having a sense of humor at the workplace and sharing jokes or funny stories with coworkers

can be a healthy release for stress on the job, but when the jokes and humor take a sexual turn, it is no longer a laughing matter. Whenever you see the office clown become the "dirty jokester," including the passing around of lewd or suggestive written anecdotes, it is time to have a chat about promptly ending the behavior. Otherwise, the joke may be on you, and not too funny, as you defend a sexual harassment claim.

2. *The close encounterer of the 3rd, 4th, and 5th kind.* This is the person who always gets uncomfortably close to coworkers when speaking with them. Face-to-face conversations should not be "in your face" and there is no need to touch your lips practically to a person's ear when speaking. The close encounter personality types need to be made aware of their body movements and language, and how others might interpret them.

3. *The "touchy-feeler."* These are people who actually touch others—an arm around the shoulder, a grasping hand, a pat on the back—when they are having a conversation and the circumstances do not call for physical contact. Congratulating someone on their promotion with a pat on the back is one thing, but giving a bear hug or rubbing someone's arm when discussing the company's latest sales figures is something altogether different. This "too close for comfort" scenario can lead to big problems. The general rule at any workplace should be "don't touch."

4. *The office gossip.* Every workplace has a rumor mill and usually a handful of employees who keep it churning. As a manager, you need to be perceptive and try to separate fact from fiction, particularly when the office gossip centers around sexual matters or the newest office romance. While gossip should always be discouraged, a manager may be tipped off to some potentially illegal behavior. Unfortunately, where there's smoke, there may be fire, and the savvy manager needs to know when and how to put it out.

5. *The sexual braggart.* The workplace is no place to discuss sexual conquests or to brag about one's accumulated scores of telephone numbers. The sexual braggart is usually an insecure attention seeker who has the capacity to offend more people

than he or she could ever hope to impress. These personality types should be told to confine their discussions to non-coworkers.

6. *The "sexual enquirer."* Unlike the sexual braggart, these individuals don't necessarily brag about their sexual exploits, but rather can't seem to have a conversation without turning it into a sexual quiz, asking coworkers about their sex lives. Like the *National Enquirer* magazine, these individuals live by the motto that "enquiring minds want to know." Managers who become aware of this inappropriate behavior should quickly instruct the offending employee that the company motto is, "Mind your own business."

7. *The cusser.* People who constantly use four-letter words, many with sexual connotations, clearly are not behaving in a professional manner and are likely to offend even the more thick-skinned employees. While not sexual harassment in and of itself, the use of foul, sexually explicit language could lead to more serious offensive conduct and should be stopped immediately.

8. *The after-work socializer.* Socializing with coworkers after a long day at the office is usually harmless and even encouraged at many companies. But when an employee persistently targets one or two coworkers with an invitation for after-work cocktails or some other similar activity, and those coworkers are consistently unreceptive, trouble may be brewing. Keep in mind that workplace sexual harassment is not confined to the workplace alone. Many cases involve situations where the harassment occurs away from the office (e.g., business trips, social functions) and legal liability is still imposed.

9. *The date baiter.* This individual constantly asks coworkers out on dates. The requests are relentless, even when the targeted person refuses. Clearly, allowing this type of behavior can lead to a classic case of the "unwanted sexual advance," and allowing it to fester is only asking for big trouble.

10. *The poster, pinup, or picture purveyor.* Pictures, posters, or other visual or written materials of a sexual nature should be prohibited. Even items less sexually provocative than the *Play-*

boy or *Playgirl* centerfolds should be banned from desks, bulletin boards, and lunchrooms, and a professional, businesslike atmosphere should be maintained at all times. Employees who don't comply can always find work at the nearest adult bookstore.

Can a Manager Be Held Personally Liable for Sexual Harassment?

As a manager, you are probably asking yourself at this point whether you can personally be sued and held legally responsible for sexual harassment, separate and apart from any legal liability imposed on your company. This is a loaded question with loaded answers. The short answer is no, at least for purposes of a sexual harassment case brought under Title VII. This is because Title VII permits an individual to sue only an "employer," which is defined under the statute as a person or entity with fifteen or more employees.[13] Thus, the general rule, supported by the vast majority of federal courts, is that if an individual does not otherwise qualify as an "employer" by personally maintaining fifteen or more employees, that individual cannot be held personally liable for sexual harassment under Title VII.[14]

But the question of a manager's personal liability for sexual harassment does not stop with the answer under Title VII. You can be on the hook under a state's antidiscrimination laws. For example, both New York's Human Rights Law and the Illinois Human Rights Act impose personal liability on managers and supervisors for sexual harassment.[15] If you live in these or other states with similar laws, you can surely expect to be named as a codefendant. Similarly, you could be sued under a state's "common law" for such things as assault and battery, infliction of emotional distress, and a slew of other civil actions related to sexual harassing conduct and often tacked onto a plaintiff's Title VII complaint in federal court. You may even be subject to criminal liability for criminal sexual assault, depending on the severity of the conduct.

The point is never to underestimate the creative mind of a hungry lawyer or the anger that may surface in a victim of sexual harassment. The "deep-pocket" defendant (e.g., your company) simply may not be enough for an aggrieved employee and your name can easily appear on a court complaint. Finally, never forget that your action or inaction with respect to sexual harassment could also have far-reaching negative effects on your own job security and career, in addition to potential legal troubles.

A Manager's Checklist for Identifying and Defending Sexual Harassment Claims

Wading through all the information presented in this chapter may seem like a formidable task. The following checklist should help you identify sexual harassment and recognize what, if any, defenses you may be able to raise.

Identify the Type of Harassment (Knew or Should Have Known)

- ❏ Quid pro quo (this for that)?
- ❏ Request for sexual favors?
- ❏ Adverse employment action?
- ❏ Hostile environment (severe and pervasive)?
- ❏ Repeated and continuous?
- ❏ Threats?
- ❏ Frequent jokes, derogatory statements, gestures, or written material of a sexual nature?
- ❏ Physical contact?
- ❏ Supervisor, coworker, or nonemployee?
- ❏ Would a "reasonable person" consider the conduct to be sexually hostile and abusive?

Consider the Defenses

- ❏ Not unwelcome
- ❏ Did employee invite or solicit?
- ❏ Did employee join in?
- ❏ Did employee complain to management?
- ❏ Did employee complain to coworkers?
- ❏ Not severe or pervasive.
- ❏ Both of the following: Company has preventive measures in place, took prompt, corrective action **and** employee failed to use preventive or corrective measures or otherwise to avoid harm.

Answers to "Test Your Knowledge"

1. *If someone doesn't complain about being sexually harassed and you, as the manager, don't know about it, your company cannot be held legally responsible.*

FALSE. The fact that someone may not complain about sexual harassment does not mean that an employer cannot be held legally responsible. In quid pro quo cases, if an employee is asked for sex and fired if he or she refuses, there is no question that sexual harassment has occurred, even if the employee never complained about it. In hostile environment cases, managers have an obligation to be on the lookout for sexually harassing behavior. Although recent Supreme Court decisions say that part of an employer's defense to hostile environment claims is to show that the employee "unreasonably failed" to correct or avoid harm (e.g., failing to complain), there may be situations where it might not be considered unreasonable for the employee to keep silent (e.g., policy says complain first to supervisor and supervisor is the alleged harasser). Additionally, the lewd sexual comments or other inappropriate sexual conduct may be so pervasive that someone would have to be "deaf, dumb, and blind" not to notice it. In those cases, the fact that the alleged victim did not complain will have no persuasive value when defending against a hostile-environment complaint.

2. *A manager cannot be held personally liable or have to pay damages for proved sexual harassment. Only the company can be proved liable.*

FALSE. Although the courts have concluded that a manager cannot be held personally responsible under federal antidiscrimination laws (e.g., Title VII), some state sexual harassment laws impose liability on agents of the employer (e.g., managers), and an employee can also sue the manager for such things as assault or battery when the sexual harassment involves inappropriate touching.

3. *In order to win a sexual harassment case alleging a sexually hostile work environment, an employee has to prove that some adverse employment action was taken against him or her (e.g., discharge, demotion, pay cut).*

FALSE. In hostile-environment sexual harassment cases, no adverse employment action has to be proved because the hostile environment alone is considered to affect an employee's work performance and other conditions of employment adversely.

4. *If someone participates in sexually offensive behavior, the person cannot claim that he or she was sexually harassed.*

FALSE. The fact that an individual may participate in sexually offensive conduct does not always insulate an employer from liability if that individual later sues for sexual harassment because he or she may still be able to establish that the conduct was "unwelcome." For instance, the individual may allege to a sympathetic jury that he felt compelled to join in because he feared losing his job or some other benefit if he did not. He may also establish that he often told coworkers to stop, but when they refused, he felt he had no choice but to play along.

5. *A company can be liable for sexual harassment only when a manager or company official engages in sexually offensive conduct toward a subordinate.*

FALSE. An employer can be liable for sexual harassment that occurs between coworkers with no management involvement. It can also be held liable when a manager sexually harasses another manager or when a customer, vendor, or other nonemployee sexually harasses one of its workers.

6. *It is illegal for a company not to have a written sexual harassment policy with a complaint procedure.*

FALSE. It is not illegal not to have a written sexual harassment policy with a complaint procedure, but it is irresponsible (and just plain stupid) if you are ever trying to defend yourself against a sexual harassment complaint. Recent Supreme Court decisions make it clear that an employer's defense to sexual harassment first requires a showing that it took appropriate preventive action. Without a firm written policy prohibiting sexual harassment and giving employees an appropriate means for complaining, there is no way that a company can show it took the proper steps to prevent sexual harassment in the workplace.

7. *A man cannot sexually harass another man, nor can a woman sexually harass another woman.*

FALSE. A man can sexually harass a man and a woman can sexually harass another woman. Additionally, a person's sexual orientation has absolutely no bearing on whether same-sex sexual harassment has occurred.

8. *A sexual harassment policy must state that employees are to report any sexually harassing conduct first to their immediate supervisor.*

FALSE. Although a sexual harassment policy should designate someone with management authority to take in sexual harassment complaints, an immediate supervisor should not be the only person designated. Often the immediate supervisor can be the alleged harasser. Therefore, the immediate supervisor and at least one additional management representative should be designated.

9. *It is sexual harassment if a manager says to a subordinate, "Wow, you really look sexy today."*

FALSE. While totally inappropriate and perhaps sexually offensive, making such a comment would not be deemed sexual harassment. It would not qualify as quid pro quo because there was no request for sexual favors and no adverse employment action was taken. Nor would it qualify as hostile-environment sexual harassment because it is one isolated sexual comment and would not meet the "severe and pervasive" standard.

10. *The following conduct by a manager will always be considered sexual harassment.*

(This is really a trick question) All of the managers' conduct identified in this question is clearly inappropriate, and even though each type of conduct, standing alone, may not be illegal, it would surely be used as evidence of sexual harassment if a complaint were made. The best and only advice is to refrain from engaging in any of the conduct identified in this question so that sexual harassment never becomes an issue. Some specific comments about each situation should also be noted.

a. *Lydia, a supervisor in an auto shop, uses sexual terms and four-letter words to express herself whenever speaking to mechanics in the shop.*

Using an occasional sexual term or four-letter word may not legally be sexual harassment, but constant use of foul language or sexual terms can do nothing but eventually get the speaker into trouble. It can be offensive to almost anyone.

b. *Gerard, a sales manager, often tells sexual jokes to his subordinates.*

Managers should be setting the example to take sexually offensive conduct out of the workplace. Sexual jokes may not be funny to everyone. The best advice is to refrain from all humor and commentary that involves a person's sex or any other class of individuals (e.g., race, religion).

c. *Denise, a vice president of an accounting firm, always gives her secretary the "once-over" with sexually suggestive eye contact when having a conversation.*

Eye contact should be with the eyes, not anywhere below the neck. Looking at someone's body parts can make them feel extremely uncomfortable and paves the way for a hostile environment claim.

d. *Sharon, a bank manager, keeps asking Marty, the receptionist, out for a date and drinks after work, telling him he needs a "real woman."*

Dating a subordinate is not illegal, but it can lead to trouble and should be avoided. What happens if the romance goes sour? The manager is simply setting herself up for a sexual harassment claim.

e. *Don, a computer software manager, keeps nude centerfolds up on the wall in his office.*

Sexual images, pictures, cartoons, or any other graphic sexual materials should be off-limits in the workplace. Anyone who wants to read and swoon over the nude centerfolds should do it in the privacy of his or her own home, not at the office.

f. *Alyse, a partner in a law firm, tells Jack, a law associate, that he "looks fantastic" and has a "great butt."*

Telling someone he or she looks fantastic or great is, of course, not illegal. Making comments about someone's body or even one's own, however, starts to cross the line. Comments about a person's sexual attributes should never be made. If compliments are in order, by all means make them. But when compliments start hinting of sexual matters, you are swimming in dangerous waters.

g. *Darek, a customer service manager, touches his employees' shoulders and moves his body very close to them whenever having a conversation.*
   If you happen to be the type of person who unconsciously touches people on the arm or shoulder when you speak with them, start becoming conscious of your actions and resist. Seemingly harmless touching can get you into trouble, so limit your physical contact on the job to a handshake.

h. *Geoff, the manager of a dental office, passes around sexually explicit jokes, cartoons, and pictures to employees in the office.*
   If the material is sexual in nature, it does not belong in the workplace.

i. *Debra, a grocery store manager, keeps asking Jerry, a meat cutter she supervises, to spend the night with her. After several requests, he finally gives in, and they have sex regularly over a three-month period.*
   Asking a subordinate to sleep with you, even if he agrees, is definitely off-limits. It may be extremely difficult to prove that an alleged office romance was consensual. Even if it can be proved and the request for sex was not conditioned on some adverse employment action (e.g., "say no and you're fired"), you may weasel your way out of a sexual harassment claim, but you are still asking for big trouble by asking any subordinate or coemployee for sex.

Case Scenarios and Practical Guidance for the Real World

Scenario A

Your organization has offices around the world, and many of your employees working in the United States are of South American and European origin. Some of these employees repeatedly kiss each other hello. Even the CEO often engages in such conduct. No employee has ever complained.

Practical Guidance

With the expanding global economy and increasing workforce diversity, there will likely be many diverse cultural influences from outside the United States in your workplace. You should remain respectful of other cultures, but following customs that are in conflict with U.S. laws or company policies is a big mistake. While a "hello" kiss may not amount to sexual harassment, clearly any employee in the U.S. workplace has a right to be free of unwanted kisses of any kind, regardless of a coworker's intent. The best course of action is to avoid kissing of any type in the workplace.

The absence of complaints about such behavior does not necessarily mean all is well. You have a responsibility to take action and should do so by speaking privately to the initiators and explain that a handshake, eye contact, and a warm verbal welcome will convey the same welcoming sentiments. Sexual harassment awareness training can also reinforce this message by clarifying the distinction between respect for cultural differences and the avoidance of inappropriate workplace behaviors. Additionally, if you are about to be on the receiving end of an unwanted kiss, you can tell the individual directly that you would prefer not to be kissed, or there are some nonverbal steps you can take to avoid it. For example, stand erect, extend your hand immediately, and avoid leaning in toward the other person.

Scenario B

Due to the nature of your organization and the work you do, employees are required to work in very close physical proximity. Men and women are shoulder to shoulder, and space is at a premium. Inadvertent touching is inevitable.

Practical Guidance

Whether the job environment is a trading pit on the New York Stock Exchange or a tightly packed production line, close quarters are a reality for some jobs. The best preemptive action is to advise employees at the time of hire about the working conditions and alert them to possible physical contact, which may be unavoidable. If this is a problem for a prospective employee, perhaps the person should be encouraged to find another job.

Additionally, the company should offer training to its existing workforce that will empower employees to speak up if they feel uncomfortable and to report their concerns to management if they don't want to handle the situation on their own. Appropriate training can also increase awareness about physical contact that is improper and that which is unavoidable. The point is to take preemptive action before a problem escalates.

Scenario C

You work for a small company of about twenty-five employees. Your "star" salesperson is a terrible flirt. Although no one has made a complaint, you have observed several women staff members roll their eyes whenever he comes near them.

Practical Guidance

Don't wait for someone to complain. You notice a potential problem from the body language you observed. Take the salesperson aside, and let him know what you saw; refer to the company's sexual harassment prevention policy, and tell him to stop the behavior because it could be sexually offensive to some of his coworkers. Remember, you must address sexual harassment whether it is reported by an employee as a complaint or merely observed by you to be inappropriate behavior.

Scenario D

You are a manager at a small retail store selling to a primarily male clientele, and you employ several attractive females. The company prides itself on personal service, and when customers come in they tend to compliment the women on their appearance. No one has complained, and the atmosphere in the store is good. However, you have overheard some of the customers make complimentary remarks about the employees' legs and "lovely figures."

Practical Guidance

You have two issues to deal with here. First, you must deal with your employees even if they have not complained. A compliment without sexual overtones is not a problem, but frequent comments about appearance, especially when they involve legs, physiques, or other body parts, can quickly fall into the unwanted category and lead to a complaint of hostile-environment sexual harassment.

Review your sexual harassment prevention policy with the employees. Emphasize that all employees are entitled to work in an environment free of sexual harassment from employees or customers. Let them know that the company will take appropriate action to correct the problem. Moreover, never allow an employee to think that "the customer is always right" when it comes to sexual harassment, even if this is your company motto.

The second issue is how to deal with the customers who have made inappropriate comments. You should approach the customers privately and explain that the company is committed to following the law with respect to sexual harassment and that you would appreciate their cooperation in that regard to avoid any potential problems. Explain that while the compliments may sound flattering, the company could be subjected to legal liability if they are unsolicited or "unwelcome." Ask the customers to please refrain from making anything other than general, nonsexual compliments.

Notes

1. 42 U.S.C. sec. 2000e et seq.
2. 42 U.S.C. sec. 2000e-2(a)(1).
3. 29 CFR sec. 1604.11(a)(1980).
4. *Burlington Industries v. Ellerth*, ___ U.S. ___; 118 S. Ct. 2365 (1998); *Faragher v. City of Boca Raton*, ___ U.S. ___; 118 S. Ct. 2275 (1998).
5. 477 U.S. 57 (1986).
6. 510 U.S. 17 (1993).
7. 29 CFR sec. 1604.11(c) (1980).
8. ___ U.S. ___; 118 S. Ct. 2365 (1998); ___ U.S. ___; 118 S. Ct. 2275 (1998).
9. 29 CFR sec. 1604.11(d) (1980).
10. 29 CFR sec. 1604.11(e) (1980).
11. See, e.g., *EEOC v. Sage Realty Corp.*, 507 F. Supp. 599 (S.D.N.Y. 1981).
12. ___ U.S. ___; 118 S. Ct. 998 (1998).
13. 42 U.S.C. sec. 2000e-2(a).
14. See, e.g., *Wathen v. General Electric Company*, 115 F.3d 400 (6th Cir. 1997); *Gary v. Long*, 59 F.3d 1391 (D.C. Cir. 1995); *Tomka v. Seiler Corporation*, 66 F.3d 1295 (2nd Cir. 1995).
15. N.Y. Exec. Law sec. 296(6); 775 ILCS 5/2-101(B)(1)(b).

CHAPTER 2

"When It's Important, Write It Down!"

Implementing an Effective Sexual Harassment Prevention Policy

I n the light of the recent Supreme Court decisions limiting the defenses to a hostile-environment sexual harassment claim, it is now more important than ever to have a comprehensive sexual harassment prevention policy. Managers need to be familiar with the essential elements of such a policy and to understand that it is the first line of defense for any hostile-environment sexual harassment claim.

You will recall from Chapter 1 that in the quid pro quo situation (a tangible job penalty for refusing sexual advances), there are basically no defenses; absolute liability is imposed. In hostile-environment cases, however, the U.S. Supreme Court gave companies two avenues of escape, both of which must be met in order to avoid liability. First, a company must show that it exercised "reasonable care" to prevent and promptly correct sexually harassing behavior. Second, a company must show that the complaining individual unreasonably failed to take advantage of the preventive or corrective measures that the company offered.

Without a bullet-proof policy in place, a company will be hard-pressed to establish that it exercised reasonable care to prevent illegal behavior or that an alleged victim did not take advantage of preventive measures. Additionally, even if a company is found liable for hostile-environment sexual harassment, the fact that it has a comprehensive sexual harassment policy may help decrease any money damages claimed by the alleged victim. Finally, an effective policy, coupled with a sound prevention program, is the only way that a company can set the tone for its workforce and realistically proclaim that sexual harassment will not be tolerated. On the other hand, not having an adequate sexual harassment policy sends the wrong message to employees and is the death knell for any company or manager dragged into court in a sexual harassment case.

Test Your Knowledge

Even if your company has a sexual harassment prevention policy, you should ask yourself whether the policy is adequate. Policies drafted five or ten years ago, or even one year ago, may not adequately address the issues that can help get you off the hook if you are sued for sexual harassment. Take the following true-or-false test now, putting a T (for true) or an F (for false) next to each statement, and then take it again after you have read the rest of this chapter. You may be surprised to learn that your company's policy needs some work.

True or False?

_____ A sexual harassment policy must be in writing in order to be legal.

_____ If a policy provides a legal definition of sexual harassment, specific examples of sexually harassing behavior need not be listed.

_____ A manager has a legal duty to report any incident that he or she believes to be inappropriate sexual conduct, even if it is not believed to be "sexual harassment."

_____ A company must never allow the direct supervisor of a complaining individual to investigate a claim of sexual harassment.

_____ A manager must abide by a complaining employee's request to refrain from taking any action or investigating a claim of sexual harassment.

_____ A sexual harassment policy must state that all employees, including managers, will receive training on sexual harassment avoidance.

_____ It is inappropriate for a manager or human resources professional of the opposite sex to take a complaint and investigate an employee's sexual harassment claim.

_____ A sexual harassment policy is not legally effective unless an employee signs a form stating that he or she has received it.

_____ An alleged victim's complaint of sexual harassment must be made in writing.

_____ Anyone found guilty of sexual harassment should be terminated in most cases.

"WAR" Games: Developing a Clear and Concise Sexual Harassment Prevention Policy

Even as far back as 1980, the EEOC guidelines on sexual harassment stressed the critical importance of a comprehensive prevention program, instructing employers to:

> take all steps necessary to prevent sexual harassment from occurring, such as affirmatively raising the subject, expressing strong disapproval, developing appropriate sanctions, informing employees of their right to raise and how to raise the issues of harassment under Title VII, and developing methods to sensitize all concerned.[1]

You may recall from Chapter 1 that the Supreme Court admonished Mechelle Vinson's employer because although it had a policy against employment discrimination in general, it did not specifically inform employees about sexual harassment.[2] More recently, the Supreme Court virtually stripped Beth Ann Faragher's employer of any defense, in part because its sexual harassment policy was not disseminated to employees.[3]

The EEOC and the Supreme Court have put employers on notice that in order to have any chance of successfully defending against a sexual harassment complaint, they must have a clear and concise sexual harassment policy properly distributed to employees. In developing such a policy, a company needs to declare "WAR." In other words, an effective policy must be Written, Accurate, and Readable. Anything short of developing a policy with these three critical components will result in a meaningless sexual harassment prevention program.

The Written Declaration of "WAR"

Perhaps the most frequently asked question about sexual harassment policies is, "Does the policy have to be in writing in order to be legal?" Technically, the answer is no. But from a practical and defense standpoint, the answer is a resounding yes! Without a written policy that is properly distributed to employees, a company cannot even begin to defend itself against a sexual harassment complaint when the company must prove initially that it acted reasonably to prevent sexual harassment. There is absolutely no way that a verbal proclamation against sexual harassment will be able to cover all the essential points needed to show that the company did act reasonably.

The Accurate "WAR" Plan

Any written sexual harassment policy has to be impeccably accurate in defining what constitutes sexual harassment and the way in which a company will investigate and remedy legitimate complaints. Defining quid pro quo, hostile environment, and covering all the legal bases is a must. Companies need to keep up with the law so that a new policy, or one that is already in place, does not miss key legal requirements. If a sexual harassment policy is not accurate with respect to the law, it will be of little use when an airtight defense plan is needed most.

The Readable "WAR" Map

A written sexual harassment prevention policy must use "reader-friendly" language, not legal gibberish, so that employees know what the policy actually means. Terms like *quid pro quo, hostile environment*, and *severe and pervasive* can be incorporated, but they must be explained in everyday language. Depending on the workforce, it may even be advisable to have the policy translated into other languages so that all employees, regardless of their ability to read English, will understand it.

Often a company will hire a lawyer to draft the policy, without meaningful participation by human resources professionals or even front-line managers. This sometimes results in a legally correct but highly technical policy. Although lawyers need to be consulted so that the policy will pass legal scrutiny, companies should avoid boilerplate language and legalese that may leave readers scratching their heads.

As a final note, even if you have no input into the development of your company's sexual harassment policy, if one exists, you should at least review it for compliance with "WAR."

The Sexual Harassment Prevention Policy: "Top Ten" List

The following elements make the "top ten" list for any sexual harassment policy. They should be included for maximum protection. Anything less may put you and your company at risk.

Zero Tolerance Statement

A zero tolerance statement should be the first element in your policy because it will clearly set the tone for the other policy statements that follow. Your company, and you personally, must set an example by aggressively conveying the message that sexual harassment is strictly prohibited and will never be tolerated in any form. It is even advisable to go one step further by including a statement that no inappropriate sexual conduct will be tolerated, even if it does not rise to the level of sexual harassment in the legal sense. Sing it loud and clear and practice it every day with your workforce, remembering that *zero tolerance* means "never."

In addition, an effective policy should include a more general statement that the company is committed to maintaining a workplace free from all types of employment discrimination and harassment, including such conduct based on sex, race, age, religion, and similar other categories. Check with your legal counsel and determine which categories of employees are considered to be a protected class for purposes of employment discrimination under both federal and state laws. City and county ordinances should also be reviewed because they sometimes prohibit other forms of employment discrimination, based on such things as sexual orientation or marital status, which may not be included in a federal or state statute. List them all in the policy.

Finally, a zero tolerance statement should use language that stresses the company's commitment to treat each and every individual, from the boardroom to the mailroom, with respect and dignity. By extolling respect and dignity in writing, and by practicing those virtues as part of a corporate philosophy, employees will feel more confident that the company is not simply paying lip service to the prevention of sexual harassment and employment discrimination in general.

Definition of Sexual Harassment

You have most likely realized that there are no quick and easy defin-itions for sexual harassment. Nevertheless, any definition in your policy has to be as simple as possible without missing the important legal points:

- Sexual harassment is against the law.

- Any conduct of a sexual nature with or between coworkers or other managers could be considered sexual harassment.

- Anyone who breaks the law will be punished.

Every sexual harassment policy should clearly explain that sex-ual harassment is a form of sex discrimination that is illegal under federal employment discrimination laws (Title VII of the Civil Rights Act of 1964) and most state antidiscrimination laws. It should also cite any city or county ordinances that also prohibit and protect against sexual harassment.

Next, the EEOC guidelines on sexual harassment should be incorporated. Many companies use them in their policies because they give a fairly accurate and clear legal definition of sexual harass-ment. They also provide the legal framework by which most courts analyze and decide sexual harassment cases. These guidelines should be reprinted in the policy with little, if any, revision, stating that they were issued by the EEOC.

No definition of sexual harassment should stop with the EEOC guidelines, however. They are only the cornerstone for a clear and concise definition. The different types of sexual harassment must be clearly identified and explained in easily understood language. For example, tell employees that a manager who promotes or fires someone based on the person's acceptance or rejection of a sexual request is engaging in quid pro quo sexual harassment, which is ille-gal and actionable in court. Explain that sexual jokes, innuendos, stereotypes, or touching can create a sexually hostile environment, which the law presumes will have an adverse effect on an individ-ual's work performance and conditions of employment. State that sexual harassment can occur between members of the same sex and that hostile-environment sexual harassment is not confined to a manager's sexual behavior; coworkers, customers, and vendors can also be the culprits. Tell the workforce that even individuals who are not the direct recipient of sexually harassing behavior can still have a legal claim because the conduct can affect their performance and working conditions.

Finally, it is essential to explain "unwelcome" sexual conduct as part of the definition of sexual harassment. This concept is often difficult to convey because it is not always apparent that certain sexual behaviors are unwanted. Use words like *unwanted, uninvited, unsolicited,* and *unencouraged.* Explain that although people's perceptions differ, it is the direct recipient of or the witness to sexually offensive conduct who is entitled to make the determination that the conduct was unwanted. Simply because one person does not find certain behaviors offensive does not mean the next person will have the same opinion. Thus, it is important to state that even sexual jokes or innuendos meant with no ill intentions can still be perceived as sexual harassment and be unwanted by the recipient or witness.

Examples of Prohibited Conduct

Every policy must give clear examples of prohibited conduct that will or could be considered sexual harassment. For instance, give the example that suggestive remarks about someone's appearance or body parts or sexual insults will not be tolerated. Explain that non-verbal behaviors such as sexual graffiti, pictures, posters, or other graphic materials of a sexual nature are unacceptable in the workplace. Finally, stress that any physical touching or contact, including patting or brushing against someone's body intentionally, is grounds for discipline up to and including discharge.

It is also a good idea to give examples of prohibited conduct that can arise through the use of office technology. Computers and all the other modern conveniences of the workplace are fertile ground for sexually offensive behaviors if privileges are abused. Every company's sexual harassment policy should state that e-mail, facsimile machines, and telephone voice-mail systems are off-limits for non-work-related use. In other words, prohibit the use of these technologies for anything but business, and stress that sending sexual jokes or other sexual communications will never be justified or tolerated, no matter what the circumstances.

Finally, in formulating a policy of zero tolerance, many companies give concrete examples of sexual harassment by listing prohibited conduct that may not rise to the level of sexual harassment but could be grounds for discipline nevertheless. In this way, a company sets its standard higher than the legal norm, and employees get the message that any questionable conduct with sexual overtones is taboo. For example, the policy may state that any joking of a sexual nature is prohibited. Such conduct may not be sexual harassment if it involves isolated remarks that are not repeated and continuous. However, a policy that prohibits even the casual sexual joke will ensure that the sexual harassment policy is taken more seriously by the workforce as a whole and assist managers with preventing more serious infractions that could amount to sexual harassment.

Duties and Responsibilities

To prevent and deal with sexual harassment effectively in the workplace, a company's sexual harassment policy should state that every person in the organization has a duty to report questionable sexual conduct promptly, a responsibility not to engage in sexual harassment, and an obligation to ensure that others, including customers, vendors, or visitors, do not engage in such conduct. Employees should be encouraged to speak up when they observe sexual harassment or any other sexual conduct that they believe to be inappropriate. The policy should stress that communication and dialogue among the workforce are essential to implementing an effective sexual harassment prevention policy.

Sound an alarm that the duty to report kicks in regardless of the offender's position and even when the individual believes that the sexual conduct is harmless or inoffensive to anyone. Encourage employees to ask questions and raise concerns about sexual harassment even if they have not witnessed a questionable event. Open communication is the key, but stress that management will make the ultimate decision as to whether the reported conduct deserves further attention.

Management also must be extremely sensitive to the way in which any disclosures from the rank and file about inappropriate sexual conduct are handled. Tell employees that they need not be afraid to report suspicious conduct and that no information will be dismissed as trivial or foolish. For individuals who may feel uncomfortable discussing their observations face-to-face with management, a sexual harassment hot line that will guarantee anonymity can be implemented. Stress that follow-up action, if any, will be handled by management in a prompt, discreet, and professional manner.

Many employees may feel that the company is encouraging a tattletale or "police state" mentality by imposing duties and responsibilities to report inappropriate behaviors. However, every individual in the organization must recognize that the war against sexual harassment has to be a group effort. Otherwise, many employees will simply see it as a management problem and ignore events that may not involve them directly. A company can have no accountability for sexual harassment if the overall corporate culture accepts the attitude that "it isn't my problem." The fact is that sexual harassment is everybody's problem, and a company needs to stress this crucial point in its policy and repeat it to the workforce at every opportunity.

Without a group effort, the sexual harassment battle will be harder fought and harder to win. Although some employees may not take their reporting duties and responsibilities seriously, many will feel compelled to assist. Even if one employee steps up to the plate with some helpful information early on, a company may have one less sexual harassment lawsuit to defend.

No Retaliation

No sexual harassment policy is acceptable without a firm statement against retaliation for employees who report inappropriate sexual conduct or assist in its prevention. Title VII of the Civil Rights Act specifically protects an employee from retaliation when "he has opposed any practice made an unlawful employment practice by [Title VII], or because he has made a charge, testified, assisted, or participated in any manner in an investigation, proceeding, or hearing [under Title VII]."

This basically means that if an employee reports or files a complaint of sexual harassment internally with an employer, or a formal charge with the EEOC, the employer cannot take any adverse employment action against that employee for doing so. In other words, if someone lodges a complaint, any discipline that might be imposed against that employee within a reasonable time frame will be closely scrutinized by the EEOC or a court if the employee alleges that the actions were taken because he or she complained. Therefore, managers must be able to justify any discipline against a complaining employee with legitimate reasons and flawless documentation.

A prohibition against retaliation should tie in with the policy statement requiring all employees to report inappropriate sexual conduct. Employees must be assured that they will suffer absolutely no repercussions from reporting, assisting, or participating in an investigation concerning sexual harassment. The policy statement should clearly state that any retaliation is unlawful, it will be strictly prohibited, and anyone determined to have engaged in unlawful retaliation will be promptly punished. The policy should again include a statement that sexual harassment complaints are encouraged and will be addressed promptly by management.

Without a clearly stated no-retaliation policy that encourages employees to come forward with complaints, a company will have a tough time proving the two components of the affirmative defense available in cases of hostile-environment sexual harassment. As you will recall from Chapter 1, an employer must basically show that it had preventive and corrective measures in place and that the employee failed to take advantage of those measures. An employee suing for sexual harassment may claim that he or she did not use the company's procedures for fear of retaliation or due to embarrassment. By not having a policy that can at least begin to counter these types of allegations, a company's defense will be severely hampered.

Complaint Procedure

At the heart of any sexual harassment prevention policy is a carefully crafted complaint procedure. Employees need to know exactly what to do and where to go if they experience or observe sexual harassment. Simply stating that complaints are encouraged and that all inappropriate sexual conduct should be reported to management is not enough. A complaint procedure must be hassle free, with easy and direct access to management, multiple options for lodging complaints, and no obstacles to open communication.

The first and most important element for an effective complaint procedure is to create a hassle-free system that gives employees ample choices. The most common mistake employers make when developing a sexual harassment complaint procedure is to state that

"sexual harassment complaints should be made to your manager."
This is simply wrong for a multitude of reasons. What if "your manager" is the sexual harasser? What if "your manager" is on vacation
for two weeks? What if you don't have a very good relationship with
"your manager"? What if "your manager" is difficult to approach on
any issue, let alone sexual harassment? Clearly, giving employees the
option to report sexual harassment only to their manager will not
promote or encourage complaints or provide easy access to the
complaint procedure in many circumstances.

A proper complaint procedure will permit an employee to
bypass his or her direct supervisor and make a complaint to other
management personnel designated by the company to handle sexual harassment issues. In larger organizations, this usually involves
designating representatives from upper management, the personnel or human resources department, ethics officers, or members of
a management committee. Some policies even state that an individual can lodge a complaint with any management official, including
the CEO or other executives. Even in smaller organizations, choices
can be provided. Managers from different departments can be designated, and the owner of the company should always be considered a possible choice.

Regardless of the size of the organization, the complaint procedure must state that an individual is not required to complain to a
direct supervisor first, although that can be an option. Some companies bypass the direct supervisor altogether and require that complaints be taken directly to the personnel or human resources
department. If this is the case, it needs to be clearly stated in the policy, which must specify who has responsibility for sexual harassment complaints.

The procedure must designate at least two managers other than
the direct supervisor as additional choices. There should be representatives of both sexes to take in complaints because some people
may feel comfortable discussing these issues only with members of
their own sex. The names of the individuals, their job titles, office
locations, and even telephone numbers should be set out in the policy. These items must then be periodically reviewed and updated
when necessary.

The second crucial element for an effective complaint procedure is to remove any obstacles that might deter employees from

making a complaint or engaging in open communication with management. For example, do not require that employees submit a written complaint on a form provided by the company. This restriction could turn off even the most cooperative employee because many individuals do not want to commit to anything in writing and fear that leaving a paper trail may come back to haunt them in the future.

Additionally, the complaint procedure for sexual harassment should never be tied to a general grievance procedure that may be applicable to other types of employee complaints. For example, most companies with a unionized workforce have a detailed grievance procedure that requires filing a complaint with a first-line supervisor and then proceeding to successive management levels for a resolution. Many nonunion companies also have similar general complaint procedures. These policies may work with other types of complaints, but they are too restrictive for sexual harassment claims. There should always be a separate and distinct procedure for the filing of sexual harassment claims.

Management also has a duty to hear, consider, and investigate all complaints that could potentially be sexual harassment even if an individual does not use a company's formal grievance procedure requiring written complaints. Thus, the most effective complaint procedure for sexual harassment encourages all types of information, including verbal, written, and even anonymous complaints. Moreover, there should be no restrictions on the time or place for lodging a complaint. If an employee does not feel comfortable raising the issue while at work, nothing should prevent him or her from contacting a management representative after hours or at home.

Finally, no complaint procedure is complete without advising employees of management's responsibilities with respect to reports of sexual harassment. Although management has a duty to investigate all complaints promptly, no matter how trivial or seemingly innocent, most larger companies insist that a direct supervisor taking in the initial complaint of sexual harassment should not independently begin an investigation without first advising the human resources department or senior management, depending on the structure of the organization. The manager should also tell the complaining employee that the matter will be reported to the management officials responsible for investigating the complaint.

In this way, employees will be assured that the procedure is applied consistently, without fear that some complaints may be given inadequate or incomplete attention depending on the manager who first heard it.

Investigation Procedure

If the initial complaint procedure is the heart of an effective sexual harassment prevention policy, then the investigation procedure is the soul that makes the policy work. Individuals need to know what happens once they have made a sexual harassment complaint. The investigation procedure needs to be clearly spelled out, and employees need to know that no matter what the claim, the investigation will be handled in a prompt, efficient, and consistent manner. Several issues need to be addressed.

First, the individuals who will conduct the investigation should be disclosed. Will it be the personnel or human resources department? Outside consultants? Lawyers? Regardless of the choice, all investigators must be impartial. If a company conducts investigations using its own staff, and there is no personnel or human resources department, then two or more individuals from different departments should be part of the investigation team so that a complaining individual will not have the claim investigated by someone in his or her own department. Additionally, in-house staff investigators should remain consistent so that employees will not perceive that cases are being handled differently or with any favoritism.

Second, the timing of any investigation must be stated. The policy should state that all sexual harassment complaints will be investigated promptly, meaning as soon as they are received. In addition to the legal pitfalls of putting a sexual harassment investigation on the back burner, employees will never think that management is taking sexual harassment very seriously if there is no firm statement that a complaint will be investigated immediately.

Third, the mechanics of the investigation need to be announced. State that interviews of the complaining individual, the alleged perpetrator, and any eyewitnesses may be conducted. Explain that other evidence will be gathered and assessed, including relevant documents, photographs, or any other tangible items that may shed light on the allegations. The policy should disclose that the results of the

investigation will remain confidential, shared only with those individuals who have a need to know (e.g., the complaining party, the
alleged perpetrator, and necessary management personnel).

Finally, state that in keeping with the company's commitment
to eradicate sexual harassment, the company will take prompt corrective action against any person found to have engaged in sexual
harassment, up to and including discharge.

Corrective Action

Corrective action has two components, and both need to be
explained to the workforce. First, the policy must state that a person
found to have engaged in sexual harassment will be disciplined
promptly. Prompt remedial or corrective action for the harasser is a
crucial part of any employer's defense to a hostile-environment sexual harassment claim. Employees and managers should understand
that once the investigation is complete and there is reason to believe
that sexual harassment has occurred, there will be absolutely no
delay in giving the proper discipline.

The policy should stress that the punishment will always fit the
crime. This means that the policy should identify certain options
regarding discipline, depending on the severity of the sexual harassment. For example, if someone with a perfect record to this point
has engaged in inappropriate sexual joking or stereotypical remarks
determined to be sexual harassment, termination may be too harsh
a penalty; perhaps counseling or training would be appropriate in
this case. In contrast, a physical sexual harasser (e.g., someone who
engages in offensive touching) will most likely receive the equiva-
lent of workplace capital punishment: termination.

The best policies go one step further with regard to corrective
action. In order to drive home the zero tolerance theme, management should reserve the right to discipline employees for any type
of sexual conduct that is deemed to be inappropriate in management's discretion, regardless of whether it rises to the level of sexual
harassment in the legal sense. For instance, the secretary who tells
an off-color sexual joke within the earshot of customers and other
employees deserves some discipline, even if her behavior may not
technically be sexual harassment. Such behavior is inappropriate
and unprofessional, and to let it go unchecked can only lead to
more serious problems.

Discipline for the perpetrator of sexual harassment does not end the matter. The second component of an effective policy on corrective action should never ignore the victim of sexual harassment. The policy should state that the victim will be informed of the outcome of the investigation and any discipline imposed on the perpetrator. The victim should also be permitted to submit a written statement to the human resources department or senior management if he or she is dissatisfied or disagrees with the outcome. Finally, the victim should be offered counseling or some other reasonable assistance from an employer to deal with the effects of the sexual harassment, including a possible job transfer, change in work schedule, or other appropriate assistance. Again, this should be left to management's discretion depending on the circumstances, but the workforce should be alerted to the fact that the company cares about its employees and will do whatever it can to alleviate the effects of sexual harassment as well as the offense itself.

Confidentiality

No company can print or practice an effective sexual harassment prevention policy without giving the employees involved certain assurances about confidentiality. Most victims of sexual harassment feel embarrassed or uncomfortable about lodging a complaint, and the last thing they need is to hear their experience being bounced around the lunchroom table as gossip. Someone accused of sexual harassment is obviously at a low point and has understandable concerns about his or her reputation and job future. Witnesses to sexual harassment are often afraid to come forward, especially if they are friends with the alleged victim or perpetrator; and without some assurance of confidentiality, they may look the other way and say nothing.

For all these reasons and probably others, a sexual harassment policy must state that a complaint will be kept confidential and disclosed only to the extent necessary to conduct an adequate investigation. Obviously a company cannot guarantee absolute confidentiality because it would hamper a thorough investigation. But the policy should explain that the matter will be disclosed only to those individuals with a need to know.

This means that witness statements given to an investigator for the company and other evidence will be disclosed only to the investigators and the managers who are responsible for taking proper corrective action. It does not mean that the matter is put on the agenda at the next monthly managers meeting for all to hear and discuss. Nor does it mean that a manager who first hears a complaint should report it to his or her immediate supervisor rather than reporting directly to human resources or the appropriate organizational channels.

What about the complaining employee who does not want his or her complaint disclosed to anyone or investigated at all? Although this is a troubling issue, the answer is clear. An employer has a legal duty to investigate promptly all complaints of sexual harassment regardless of an employee's request to do otherwise. Although some courts have let employers off the hook for sexual harassment when an employee requested that her complaint remain confidential and that no action be taken, this is by far the exception and not the rule. Therefore, employees must understand that confidentiality will be preserved only to the point where it does not jeopardize management's legal responsibilities.

Training Requirements

Prior to the Supreme Court's decisions in *Ellerth* and *Faragher*, few sexual harassment policies mentioned anything about training. Now, however, having a policy on training employees about sexual harassment is essential to reinforce a company's commitment to eradicating sexual harassment among the workforce and to prove that it had effective preventive and corrective measures in place when trying to defend itself in court. The policy statement can state that all employees, including management personnel, will be required to attend training sessions to assist in the identification and prevention of sexual harassment.

At least one training session should be held each year where the company's policy is reviewed and discussed, and questions are encouraged. All employees, right up to the CEO, should be trained to recognize sexual harassment, to deal with it when it occurs, and to assist management in its efforts to prevent it. Without a training requirement and program, a company's sexual harassment prevention program may be perceived by the workforce as nothing more than a paper tiger, without the muscle needed to make it effective.

Disseminate and Educate!

Once the written policy is in place, the battle against sexual harassment is far from over. Merely having a policy will do little to insulate a company from liability if the policy sits in the middle of the employee handbook and the workforce is not specifically educated about sexual harassment. You can never overeducate or spend too much time explaining the company's policy against sexual harassment to employees or management. The better you disseminate and educate, the better are your chances of winning a sexual harassment lawsuit or avoiding the filing of a complaint in the first place. The essentials of this effort are as follows.

The Distribution Network

Although the policy needs to be included in an employee handbook, it should also be issued as a separate memorandum or bulletin to the entire workforce at least twice per year. It should come from the top, meaning the chief executive officer or president of the company should distribute the policy under his or her signature. If possible, the policy should be mailed to the employees' homes with a personal letter from top management extolling the virtues of zero tolerance and the company's commitment to a workplace totally free of sexually harassing conduct. In this way, employees will take it more seriously than a run-of-the-mill policy issued by the human resources department.

The policy must be distributed to all employees: temporary employees, contract employees, part-timers, employees on a leave of absence, all levels of management, and any employees working off-site.

Signing on the Dotted Line

Many court cases have been lost because the employer did not insist that employees sign off on a sexual harassment policy. Nothing is more frustrating than knowing an employee received the policy, but he testifies in court that he never did, and there is no written proof that he is lying. It is essential that a company obtain proof by requiring every employee, right up to the CEO, to sign and date an acknowledgment form or receipt stating that he or she received the policy, read it, understood it, and agreed to abide and be bound by it.

This form must be required, as a condition of hiring or continued employment. If a potential new employee refuses to sign, the person is not worth hiring. If a current employee refuses to sign, ask the employee for his or her reasons for refusal and note those reasons on the acknowledgment form. All forms should then be placed in the employees' personnel files. Every time the sexual harassment policy is reissued, even if it has not changed, each employee must sign and date an acknowledgment form.

The Ultimate Poster Child

In addition to distributing a sexual harassment policy to each individual employee, the company should post the policy in conspicuous places at the work site. It can be enlarged and placed in a frame to distinguish it from other posted company policies. Bulletin boards in the lunchroom, near time clocks, in rest rooms, and at employee workstations are good choices for getting the message across. It is even advisable to have the policy on a coffee table or other visible area in the reception area where other reading material is placed. This will put customers, clients, vendors, and other visitors on notice that the company is serious about preventing sexual harassment, no matter what the source.

Meetings of the Minds

Because preventing sexual harassment is such a serious matter, review the policy in small group meetings with employees. These educational sessions should be led by a manager who has been trained in sexual harassment avoidance and clearly understands the company's zero tolerance policy. The employee meetings should be held during the workday shortly after the policy is distributed and posted. They should also be held each time the policy is reissued (again, twice per year), and additional small group meetings should be held periodically to heighten the workforce's awareness. Some companies use commercial videotapes about sexual harassment to give employees a firsthand look at the types of behaviors that are unacceptable. Employees should be told that attendance at these meetings is mandatory and that a sign-in sheet will be used and retained to confirm attendance. The company's sexual harassment policy must be discussed in detail, and employee questions must be answered with candor.

No Manager Immunity

Managers need to understand completely the company's sexual harassment policy and the company's zero tolerance mentality. Frequent group meetings with management personnel to discuss and review the policy are essential. More importantly, managers must be trained to recognize and deal with sexual harassment issues. They need to be educated and trained on the following matters:

- The types of conduct that constitute sexual harassment

- Their responsibility to ensure that sexual harassment does not occur

- That failure to respond will result in discipline

- The procedures for taking in a complaint, reporting to the proper channels, and investigating sexual harassment

- Methods for implementing prompt corrective action and identifying and dealing with their own behaviors that could lead to a sexual harassment claim

During any training sessions, managers need to be reminded that they may likely be sued along with the company if any sexual harassment complaint ever reaches court. Evidence of a properly trained management staff will be invaluable if a company is ever faced with a sexual harassment lawsuit because it at least establishes that a good-faith effort was made to prevent such conduct.

Putting It Together

Making sure a sexual harassment prevention policy contains all the essential elements is only part of the battle. Managers also need to know what *not* to do when preparing and then implementing a policy. Following are some common mistakes companies and managers should avoid when attempting to put a sexual harassment prevention policy in place:

✘ DON'T issue a one-paragraph policy lacking even the minimum requirements.

✗ DON'T fail to update a policy that was developed years ago.

✗ DON'T bury the policy in an employee handbook.

✗ DON'T use a generic policy that is not tailored to the specific needs or structure of the organization.

✗ DON'T limit or restrict distribution of a policy to certain offices or groups of employees.

✗ DON'T limit application of the policy to only the rank and file.

✗ DON'T fail to issue a policy because the company and its workforce are small.

✗ DON'T tolerate behaviors that contradict the policy.

✗ DON'T fail to give examples of sexual harassment in the policy.

✗ DON'T fail to "walk the talk" by ignoring managers' conduct or not following through with complaint, investigation, and corrective action procedures.

✗ DON'T ignore rude, obnoxious, or abrasive behaviors that show a complete lack of respect for others even though it may not rise to the level of sexual harassment.

✗ DON'T apply different standards for different employees, no matter who they are or how high they have climbed up the corporate ladder.

The policy shown in Exhibit 2-1 is ready-made and includes all the essential elements for an effective sexual harassment prevention policy discussed in this chapter.

Exhibit 2-1. Sample sexual harassment prevention policy and employee acknowledgment form.

TO: ALL EMPLOYEES

FROM: JACKIE JONES, CHIEF OPERATING OFFICER

RE: SEXUAL HARASSMENT PREVENTION POLICY

Our Company is committed to providing you with a workplace free from all forms of discrimination and one in which every employee is treated with honor, respect, dignity, and professionalism. To that end, the Company hereby adopts a "zero tolerance" policy against sexual harassment and any inappropriate conduct of a sexual nature by employees or managers. In addition, no form of harassment or employment discrimination will be tolerated, including discrimination based on an individual's sex, race, color, religion, national origin, disability, age, veteran status, citizenship, sexual orientation, or any other class protected by federal, state, or local laws.

Sexual harassment is sex discrimination and illegal. It is prohibited under federal law by Title VII of the Civil Rights Act of 1964, and the laws of [State]. According to the federal Equal Employment Opportunity Commission, sexual harassment includes unwelcome sexual advances, requests for sexual favors, and other verbal or physical conduct of a sexual nature when: (1) submission to such conduct is made either explicitly or implicitly a term or condition of employment; (2) submission to or rejection of such conduct is used as the basis for an employment decision affecting an employee; or (3) such conduct has the purpose or effect of unreasonably interfering with an employee's work performance or creating an intimidating, hostile, or offensive working environment.

Sexual harassment can occur between a manager and an employee, between coworkers of the opposite or same sex, and by customers or other visitors to the Company. A manager who grants an employment benefit or imposes an employment penalty based on submission to or refusal of a request for sexual favors from an employee has committed "quid pro quo" sexual harassment. Managers, employees, or visitors who engage in inappropriate sexual conduct can be held responsible for creating a sexually hostile work environment, another form of sexual harassment that is unlawful.

Even employees who are not the direct recipients of sexual harassment but witness sexually harassing behavior are indirect victims of sexual harassment.

Sexual harassment also involves sexual conduct that is "unwelcome." This means that the recipient or observer did not want, encourage, invite, or solicit the conduct. However, any conduct that is or could be perceived as personally offensive or failing to respect the rights of others could be "unwelcome." Because people perceive things differently, every employee has an obligation to refrain from any conduct of a sexual nature.

Sexual harassing conduct can include, but is not limited to, the examples provided below. However, in keeping with the Company's "zero tolerance" policy against sexual harassment, all conduct of a sexual nature is prohibited:

Exhibit 2-1 (continued)

Verbal: sexual jokes; innuendos; comments based on sexual stereotypes; sexually suggestive comments; sexual propositions; threats; whistles or cat-calls, comments about a person's body parts; and any sexual statements communicated through the Company's computer systems, fax machines, or telephones.

Nonverbal: sexual graffiti, pictures, posters, cartoons, or objects; sexual e-mail communications or jokes; eye contact with a person's sexual body parts; and obscene gestures.

Physical: any intentional uninvited physical contact, including touching, brushing up against the body, pinching, patting, and rubbing.

Sexual harassment is insulting, offensive, and demeaning. Therefore, all employees at the Company, including managers, have a duty to prevent and immediately report any conduct of a sexual nature even if they do not personally believe that the conduct amounts to sexual harassment. No reported incident will be considered too trivial, and the Company strongly encourages all employees to come forward with their observations or complaints.

In addition, no employee will be retaliated against in any manner for reporting a suspected incident of sexual harassment or for assisting the Company in its efforts to prevent such incidents from occurring.

Employees who believe they have been a victim of sexual harassment or who have observed inappropriate sexual conduct should immediately report the incident to any of the following three individuals: Jane Doe, Vice President of Human Resources; Fred Smith, Assistant Vice President; or Jackie Jones, Chief Operating Officer. They can be reached by telephone at the following numbers:_____. Under no circumstances should an employee report an incident to a member of management who he or she is alleging committed sexual harassment. If a complaint is made to a direct supervisor, the supervisor will report the incident to the individuals named above before any action is taken. Complaints can be made in person, anonymously, verbally, or in writing.

All sexual harassment complaints will be investigated promptly by one or more of the individuals named above. However, if any of the investigators are named as the alleged sexual harasser, they will not have any responsibility for conducting the investigation. The investigation may involve witness interviews and a review of any documents, objects, or other evidence related to the sexual harassment complaint.

All complaints and investigations will be kept confidential to the maximum extent possible, and in accordance with the Company's legal responsibility to conduct a prompt and adequate investigation. Only those individuals at the Company with a "need to know" will be informed.

Following the investigation, the investigators will review their findings with the appropriate managers, and a determination will be made on how the complaint should be resolved. In appropriate cases, the perpetrator will be promptly subject to discipline, up to and including discharge, in management's discretion, depending on the seriousness of the offense or other circumstances. However, the Company reserves the right to discipline any employee who engages in offensive conduct, regardless of whether sexual harassment has been found. A complaining employee will be made aware of the results of the investigation and the discipline imposed. If the complaining employee disagrees with the outcome of the investigation, he or she will have an opportunity to submit a written statement to that effect. In addition, the Company will take whatever steps are reasonably necessary to assist a victim of sexual harassment with counseling opportunities or by other means.

To further promote the Company's commitment to a "zero tolerance" policy against sexual harassment, all employees, including management personnel, will be required to attend periodic sexual harassment sensitivity and awareness training sessions to assist the Company in the identification and prevention of sexual harassment at all levels.

—————————————————
Jackie Jones, Chief Operating Officer

ACKNOWLEDGMENT FORM

I have carefully read the attached Sexual Harassment Prevention Policy, and I fully understand its meaning and content. I agree to abide by all the requirements of the Policy and to accept my responsibility to report promptly any inappropriate conduct which I may observe. I also agree that my own conduct will be subject to the Policy and that I may be disciplined, up to and including termination, if it is determined that I have engaged in any inappropriate conduct.

—————————————————
Employee's Signature and Date

Checklist for Drafting, Disseminating, and Educating on Sexual Harassment Policy

Following is a checklist of all the essential elements for drafting, disseminating, and educating the workforce on sexual harassment. Refer to this checklist both before and after developing a sexual harassment prevention policy to make sure all the points have been covered.

- ❑ Plain and "user-friendly" language
- ❑ Zero tolerance for all employees and management
- ❑ Prohibition against all forms of discrimination
- ❑ Prohibition against all inappropriate sexual conduct
- ❑ Examples of prohibited conduct
- ❑ Legal basis for sexual harassment
- ❑ Clear definition with EEOC guidelines
- ❑ Definition of *unwelcome*
- ❑ Employees' duties and responsibilities
- ❑ Encourage complaints
- ❑ No retaliation
- ❑ Complaint procedure
- ❑ Investigation procedure
- ❑ Corrective action
- ❑ Confidentiality
- ❑ Training requirements
- ❑ Distribution to all employees
- ❑ Senior executive to issue policy
- ❑ Employee acknowledgment form

Answers to "Test Your Knowledge"

1. *A sexual harassment policy must be in writing in order to be legal.*

FALSE. There is no legal requirement that a sexual harassment policy must be in writing, but any company failing to have a written policy will surely have trouble convincing the EEOC, a judge, or a jury that it implemented an adequate and reasonable preventive and corrective program when defending against a sexual harassment complaint.

2. If a policy provides a legal definition of sexual harassment, specific examples of sexually harassing behavior need not be listed.

FALSE. No definition of sexual harassment is complete without examples of inappropriate sexual conduct that could amount to sexual harassment.

3. A manager has a legal duty to report any incident that he or she believes to be inappropriate sexual conduct, even if it is not believed to be "sexual harassment."

TRUE. The EEOC and the courts have made it clear that an employer has a legal responsibility to take all steps necessary to prevent, promptly investigate, and correct sexual harassment. Even if an individual does not formally complain, managers have an obligation to report suspected incidents.

4. A company must never allow the direct supervisor of a complaining individual to investigate a claim of sexual harassment.

FALSE. Depending on the organizational structure, it may be appropriate for a direct supervisor to investigate a complaint of sexual harassment as long as he or she is not the alleged perpetrator. In many smaller companies, this may be the case. However, the better approach, even in smaller organizations, is to assign at least two managers who are impartial and preferably from different departments, to conduct an investigation.

5. A manager must abide by a complaining employee's request to refrain from taking any action or investigating a claim of sexual harassment.

FALSE. The general rule is that a company has a legal obligation to investigate promptly and take appropriate corrective action on any complaint of sexual harassment, regardless of an employee's request to do otherwise. However, a complaining employee should be told that confidentiality will be maintained to the greatest extent possible and that only those individuals with a "need to know" will be informed about the complaint.

6. A sexual harassment policy must state that all employees, including managers, will receive training on sexual harassment avoidance.

FALSE. There is no legal requirement that a policy has to require sexual harassment training, but the more effective policies contain this requirement in furtherance of an employer's legal obligation to inform and sensitize all employees about the issue.

7. *It is inappropriate for a manager or human resources professional of the opposite sex to take a complaint and investigate an employee's sexual harassment claim.*

FALSE. Male or female management representatives or outside consultants can be designated as a complaint intake person and investigator regardless of the sex of the complaining employee. However, an effective sexual harassment prevention policy will give the complaining employee a choice of persons of both sexes to lodge an initial complaint, and it is preferable to assign persons of both sexes to investigate.

8. *A sexual harassment policy is not legally effective unless an employee signs a form stating that he or she has received it.*

FALSE. A policy is legally effective even if a company does not insist that employees sign for it. However, failing to obtain an employee's acknowledgment that he or she received and understood the policy may come back to haunt the company in litigation. How else do you defend against an employee's claim that "I never saw any sexual harassment policy and nobody ever told me about one"?

9. *An alleged victim's complaint of sexual harassment must be made in writing.*

FALSE. Employees cannot be required to lodge their complaints in any particular form. Verbal and written complaints must be accepted, promptly investigated, and promptly corrected. Moreover, even if an employee does not say he or she has been sexually harassed, a manager has an obligation to take action if the facts being alleged could be considered sexual harassment.

10. *Anyone found "guilty" of sexual harassment should be terminated in most cases.*

FALSE. The punishment must fit the crime. If someone is a stellar employee with no record of prior offenses and the sexual harassment was not sufficiently egregious, termination may be too harsh a penalty. Counseling and other remedies may be the better choice. However, if the offense was egregious (e.g., offensive touching) or the perpetrator has been involved in other sexually harassing conduct, termination may be the only appropriate remedy.

Case Scenarios and Practical Guidance for the Real World

Scenario A

Your sexual harassment prevention policy indicates that employees will be asked to put their sexual harassment complaints in writing. The company believes that this practice will underscore the importance of the claim, make it official, help employees understand that the company is serious about eradicating sexual harassment in the workplace, and help the employee to clarify the exact nature of the complaint. Later you hear that some employees view this as a barrier to making a claim of sexual harassment.

Practical Guidance

Your policy should present no barrier to the employee who wants to report a complaint of sexual harassment. That is the reason for a reader-friendly policy that gives employees several options for reporting a complaint. Requiring employees to reduce their complaints to writing may cause them to resist and send them into the waiting arms of lawyers, who will listen sympathetically without a writing requirement.

Although the person who conducts a sexual harassment investigation should request the employee to sign off on notes taken about the allegations, it is not a necessity that he or she do so, nor is it necessary for a complaint to be in writing for the company to take action. A complaint begins with the verbal mention that something of an unwanted sexual nature has occurred. It is official at this point. There are no unofficial complaints. A complaint is equally significant if it is made in a typed format or in a brief conversation where a third party mentions that she doesn't appreciate the dirty jokes that are exchanged by two coworkers within earshot of her desk every morning.

Scenario B

Your company culture abhors policies. The CEO issued a one-paragraph statement indicating that the company will not tolerate sexual harassment or other forms of harassment. There are concerns among your executive committee that developing a longer policy and asking everyone to sign it will just draw attention to the issue and encourage complaints.

Practical Guidance

In the case of sexual harassment, past is not necessarily prologue. One of the key elements in preventing sexual harassment is clarifying the company's expectations, which are done clearly in a comprehensive written policy. A vague or unreasonably short policy can confuse employees or create an impression that the company pays little more than lip-service to the issue. A clear, well-written policy is an excellent opportunity to prove that the company has informed all employees of their responsibilities, offers a means of reporting complaints, and will not tolerate retaliation. All of these elements will weigh in the company's favor should a sexual harassment complaint or lawsuit arise.

Notes

1. 29 C.F.R. sec. 1604.11(f) (1980).
2 *Meritor Savings Bank v. Vinson,* 477 U.S. 57 (1986).
3. *Faragher v. City of Boca Raton,* ___ U.S. ___; 118 S. Ct. 2275 (1998).

CHAPTER 3

"The Road to Hell Is Paved With Good Intentions"

Dealing With Your Own Personal Attitudes and Conduct

A s a manager, your own personal attitudes and conduct, including the way you speak, may have a much greater impact on how your workforce deals with sexual harassment than any written policy statement. Written words will never have any meaning and never be taken seriously unless management makes an effort to assess and monitor its own conduct with respect to sexual harassment. To make the words come alive, appropriate conduct has to start at the top. From the CEO right down to the first-line supervisor, every individual with a management position has to take a hard look in the mirror, recognize attitudes and behaviors that may be inappropriate, and make an ongoing commitment to change those attitudes and behaviors. With hard work and a little luck, your own self-assessment will take hold and have a powerful impact on the rank and file when issues of sexual harassment arise.

Never underestimate how your actions are perceived by the rest of the workforce. As a manager, you have to set the right example. This requires being in touch with how and why you act in a certain way while recognizing the realities of the workplace environment. Conduct that may be acceptable at a cocktail party or in your own backyard could be light-years away from conduct that is acceptable at work. Recognizing and dealing with this dichotomy is the first step toward enlightenment in your attitudes and conduct with respect to sexual harassment issues.

Moreover, all managers bring their own preconceived notions and ideas about sexual harassment to the workplace. How you were raised, your social background, and your general life experiences bring with them built-in biases and stereotypes that affect how you behave and how you react to your coworkers. Consequently, some of your actions and reactions concerning sexual harassment may be way off base and perceived as offensive, even if done with good intentions. There also may not always be a correlation between what you think, feel, or believe is proper conduct.

You need to recognize that your attitudes and conduct could have a negative effect and that fighting built-in biases and stereotypes is part of the program for change. Additionally, knowing how to recognize and act appropriately when sexual harassment moves beyond the four walls of the office, realizing how corporate culture issues have an effect, and understanding how to treat coworkers is all part of an ongoing process to help you deal with sexual harassment correctly. It takes careful thought, blunt self-criticism, and a willingness to change when change is necessary. Anything less jeopardizes your ability to deal with sexual harassment and may even impede your overall effectiveness as a manager.

Test Your Knowledge

How do personal attitudes and conduct affect your ability to deal with sexual harassment? This is a difficult question, especially when you might not even realize that you are acting in a way that some people may find offensive. Take the following true-and-false test, putting a T (for true) or an F (for false) before each statement, and try to determine what you already know about yourself and about your potential for inappropriate behavior. Answer the questions again after completing this chapter, and compare your initial answers to the answers provided at the end. You may discover that some of your initial perceptions were far afield from reality.

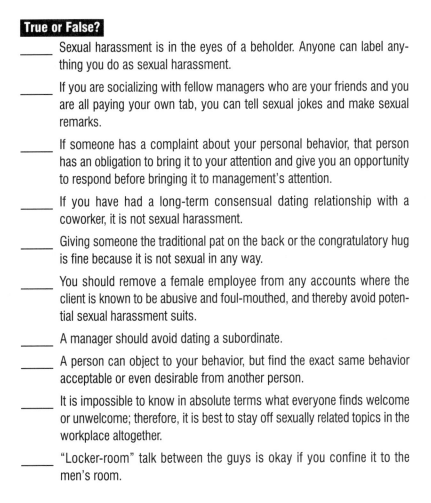

True or False?

_____ Sexual harassment is in the eyes of a beholder. Anyone can label anything you do as sexual harassment.

_____ If you are socializing with fellow managers who are your friends and you are all paying your own tab, you can tell sexual jokes and make sexual remarks.

_____ If someone has a complaint about your personal behavior, that person has an obligation to bring it to your attention and give you an opportunity to respond before bringing it to management's attention.

_____ If you have had a long-term consensual dating relationship with a coworker, it is not sexual harassment.

_____ Giving someone the traditional pat on the back or the congratulatory hug is fine because it is not sexual in any way.

_____ You should remove a female employee from any accounts where the client is known to be abusive and foul-mouthed, and thereby avoid potential sexual harassment suits.

_____ A manager should avoid dating a subordinate.

_____ A person can object to your behavior, but find the exact same behavior acceptable or even desirable from another person.

_____ It is impossible to know in absolute terms what everyone finds welcome or unwelcome; therefore, it is best to stay off sexually related topics in the workplace altogether.

_____ "Locker-room" talk between the guys is okay if you confine it to the men's room.

Dealing With Your Own Attitudes About Sexual Harassment

You probably think of yourself as a good manager who knows how to deal with employees in a fair and reasonable manner when issues arise in the workplace. Even if you have never had any experience with sexual harassment, you probably believe that you would react to that issue with the same level-headed approach. You may not know all the legal mumbo-jumbo, but no doubt you agree with the general premise that sexually harassing conduct is improper and illegal. You would also probably agree that as a manager, you would try to prevent and stop it. However, having the "right" attitudes or beliefs about sexual harassment may not be enough. You may be well intentioned, but when your own attitudes and beliefs are put to the test, they may fall short of properly dealing with the problem and could lead to trouble.

Sexual Harassment Is Wrong

Who wouldn't agree with the statement that sexual harassment is wrong? Obviously any manager who has read a newspaper will know that sexual harassment is not only wrong, but unlawful. However, even though you may have this opinion, do you really think that sexual harassment is no big deal unless someone engages in truly outrageous conduct like grabbing a coworker's private sexual parts or verbally demeaning a member of the opposite sex until the person is at the point of tears? Simply knowing that sexual harassment is wrong doesn't necessarily mean that you are prepared to deal with it in every situation.

You need to realize that sexual harassment can come in many forms. It can be extremely subtle conduct, such as when someone looks at another person in a suggestive manner, making eye contact with that person's sexual body parts. It can also come in the form of a few simple jokes about sexual matters that you and many other people may not find offensive. However, even if one person finds such conduct offensive, that person's perception will control, and the matter will need your prompt attention.

Simply understanding the basic premise that sexual harassment is wrong may still cause you to miss the fact that sexual harassment can occur when derogatory or stereotypical comments are made about members of one sex. For example, a female employee may repeatedly tell a male coworker that he is a "typical" man, constantly tell male-bashing jokes, berate him about acting "macho" and thinking that he is "God's gift to women," and make other stereotypical and derogatory comments. This may seem like harmless banter to you and many other employees, but to some men it could be considered highly offensive and adversely affect the way they do their jobs. Hence, you may have a case of hostile-environment sexual harassment on your hands when you least expect it.

The point is that simply having the attitude or belief that sexual harassment is wrong in the general sense may not be enough to prompt appropriate action when events take place that you or others may not perceive as wrong. You must be cognizant of your surroundings and make every effort to be aware of even the most subtle behaviors. If you ignore all but the most egregious conduct, you will not be doing your job to promote the company's sexual harassment prevention policy, and you could subject both the company and yourself to legal liability.

Finally, you need to continuously monitor your own conduct and refrain from engaging in any questionable behavior that could be construed as sexual harassment. For example, you may jokingly make a statement that someone will be "looking for a new job" if he or she rebuffs your requests for a date. You should never make such comments even in jest because someone may take you seriously and if the individual later does get fired, even for an unrelated reason, you could be accused of engaging in quid pro quo sexual harassment, the most serious sexual harassment offense. You and the company will have no defense. Always remember that your conduct will set the tone for the employees you supervise and others in the workplace. When your own behavior is questionable, don't expect others to act any differently.

"I'm No Sexual Harasser!"

You may truly believe that you would never sexually harass a coworker, but can you honestly say that your actions in the workplace could never be construed by anyone as sexually offensive conduct? Even the most subtle behavior can sometimes lead to a sexual harassment complaint. For example, you may be in the habit of repeating sexual jokes you hear from vendors, some of which may be offensive to others. You also may have a paternalistic attitude toward women that comes naturally to you and that you do not mean to be offensive.

Unfortunately, the way *you* characterize your actions is irrelevant. The fact that you see yourself as a friendly, playful, or fun-loving manager has no bearing on whether someone is offended by your behavior. The bottom line is that having a good heart and good intentions is no defense. It also is no defense that you are personally unaware about how someone else is perceiving your conduct.

Thus, it is extremely important to think before you act and ask yourself "Would anyone find this conduct to be offensive?" In most circumstances where anything related to sex is involved, the answer to that question will be yes. Remember, meaning no harm can still mean sexual harassment. When monitoring your own behavior, you should also ask yourself, "Would I want someone talking this way to my mother/father, son/daughter, spouse/partner?" If you are really being honest with yourself, in nine out of ten cases the answer will be no. Again, remember it is the recipient's perception, not yours, that will control the outcome of a sexual harassment complaint.

Stop Means "Stop"

Does *stop* really *mean* "stop" to you? For example, if someone tells you to stop doing something and says that it is bothersome, you will probably stop doing it. However, when it comes to sexual harassment, you may not be told to stop by the person you are offending. Remember that an alleged victim of sexual harassment basically has no obligation to lodge a complaint with you, particularly if you are the alleged harasser.

If your company follows the guidelines recommended in Chapter 2, your sexual harassment prevention policy will specifically allow for an employee to bypass a direct supervisor or other manager when complaining if that person is the subject of the sexual harassment complaint. Therefore, you may not know that your conduct was offending anyone until you are approached by senior management. Never rely on the old adage that "no news is good news" because it is simply not true that someone who finds your behavior to be offensive will always tell you about it.

Moreover, never rationalize in your own mind that your conduct is not unwelcome or acceptable simply because no objections are raised. An individual can "join in the fun" in some circumstances and still perceive your behavior as unwelcome or offensive. Many individuals are too embarrassed or uncomfortable confronting a coworker or manager when they are offended by certain behaviors. When sexual conduct or commentary is involved, never assume that what you say and do is accepted by everyone.

In some cases, an individual may tell you directly that he or she finds your behavior offensive. If that occurs, never question the employee's remark or try to persuade him or her that you "meant nothing by it." Stop the behavior immediately, and apologize on the spot. Heeding this simple advice may satisfy the offended employee and prevent a complaint of sexual harassment from going any further. You need to realize that the person who has directly complained to you about your conduct has given you a warning, and you should automatically assume that warning means your conduct is unwelcome. Consequently, be alert to how your communications are being received, and if you are not sure, ask.

These principles apply to physical contact as well. You may be naturally affectionate and often feel the need to hug someone or pat someone on the back. This is a perfect example of the double life you are forced to lead. Such actions may be totally appropriate in nonwork-related social settings or with family members, but they are off-limits in the workplace. The only proper physical conduct at the workplace is a handshake. Anything more is a risky proposition and could subject you to a sexual harassment complaint.

Living by the Golden Rule

Doing unto others as you would have others do unto you is perhaps one of the most widely accepted standards for most people's conduct, in the workplace or elsewhere. Most managers believe in this golden rule and believe that they practice what is preached. However, this standard of conduct often has no application to sexual harassment. You may personally find certain behaviors to be completely normal, acceptable, and even desirable. A sexual joke or gesture, or a generalization about one of the sexes, may be commonplace on your list of appropriate behaviors. However, that very same conduct that you find so tolerable may have exactly the opposite effect on someone else.

If you generally use four-letter words to make a point or habitually call the women in your office *sweetie*, you will be headed for trouble even though you have no problem with individuals' directing the same type of behavior your way. As frustrating as it may be, when it comes to sexual harassment, each person sets his or her own standards of behavior in terms of what is offensive. What you may think, feel, or believe is not controlling. It is what the recipient of your conduct thinks, feels, or believes that will determine whether sexual harassment has occurred.

"It's Only a Joke"

Obviously, the work environment should not be made to feel like a padded cell. Socializing, joke telling, and cultivating friendships are all part of the work experience. You, as well as other managers, may feel that sexual teasing and banter are part of this experience, particularly when you are in a highly stressful work environment and people need to let off steam. Certainly sex is part of life, and you can't escape it, no matter where you are. Nevertheless, standards acceptable in a social context or portrayed in the media are not the standards applied to the workplace.

For example, don't assume that discussing the sexual content of television programs or movies is acceptable at the workplace because everyone watches them and you are simply repeating something that you saw or heard. Clearly, subjects related to sex or those that degrade a particular gender are off-limits regardless of the source of the information. The fact that they originated with the media is not important. Everyone may watch television, but everyone may not watch or approve of the same shows that you do.

Similarly, never assume that laughing is a sign of approval for a sexual joke or conduct. Laughing can be provoked by nervousness, peer pressure, or simply a desire to please a person. Someone can laugh publicly and still feel uncomfortable or offended. Never try to gauge a person's reaction in this regard. The best course of action is to avoid doing anything that may cause you to wonder if you have offended another person. If you have to ask yourself the question, the answer is probably yes.

Any sexual remarks, pictures, jokes, or innuendo should be taboo at work. The prevalence of sexual harassment complaints over the past several years leaves little choice for any other alternative. Keep all communications and behaviors strictly professional. When you see any type of conduct that could potentially create a sexually hostile work environment, end it, and end it fast, even if you think the conduct is funny or amusing. It may be only a joke to you, but it may be something much more serious to someone else. The point is that you have to ignore your own personal tolerance for the conduct in question.

The Sympathetic Ear

As a manager who believes that sexual harassment is wrong, you would obviously be sympathetic and helpful to any employee who came forward with a legitimate sexual harassment complaint. However, based on your own perceptions and experiences, you may think that the complaint being made is ridiculous or just not sexual harassment. You need to be extremely careful when acting in the role of the sympathetic ear. If you are the recipient of a complaint in which the conduct being described could even remotely rise to the level of sexual harassment, listen carefully, and never substitute your judgment for the judgment of the complaining employee. The fact that you may think the complaint has no merit is not important. Although you may have certain opinions about the subject matter of the complaint or the complaining employee's credibility, keep them to yourself.

Your job is to hear the complaint and report it to senior management or the investigation team. In only the rarest of circumstances, such as when the facts being alleged have nothing to do with sexual behaviors, it may be appropriate to advise the complaining employee that sexual harassment is not at issue. However, even this can be risky. The best course of action is to write down the employee's allegations, report them immediately, and allow the appropriate individuals to make the final judgment. The best advice is to treat every complaint as a legitimate one.

Believe It or Not

An employee may come to you with allegations that you find unbelievable or know are false. Your first instinct will probably be to advise the employee of your reactions or to ignore the complaint. Obviously, false accusations will occasionally be made, but it is not your job to tell the complaining employee that you believe the allegations are false. Never ignore the complaint. You have a legal obligation to hear all sexual harassment complaints, even those that are obviously bogus, and to treat each with the same degree of seriousness and professionalism that you would give to the most credible claims. False complaints should be dealt with at the investigation and corrective action stages, not when you first hear about them.

A Dangerous Assumption

Many managers of both sexes really believe that for all practical purposes, sexual harassment is really all about men harassing women. This is a dangerous assumption, which most likely stems from built-in biases and stereotypes about men and women in general. Make no mistake, women can sexually harass men, and there are hundreds of court cases and EEOC proceedings to prove it. Women can be equally or more aggressive than men, and they too can cross the line from innocent comments or behaviors to inappropriate sexual conduct.

The days of men being the only ones who tell raunchy sexual jokes or aggressively pursue the opposite sex are over, if they ever existed.

In addition, men can sexually harass other men, and women can sexually harass other women. For purposes of sexual harassment, the battle of the sexes is no longer the rule of thumb. The U.S. Supreme Court made it clear in *Oncale v. Sundowner Offshore Services, Inc.* that individuals who repeatedly subject a member of their own sex to sexually offensive remarks or other conduct have engaged in hostile environment sexual harassment.[1]

Fighting Typical Stereotypes and Built-In Biases

Your attitudes, conduct, and general feelings about the specifics of sexual harassment are obviously important. However, you also bring more general stereotypes and built-in biases to the job, and they too can have an effect on how you deal with sexual harassment. It is no secret that men and women have certain beliefs about the opposite sex, some justified and others purely fiction. Most people learn to rationalize their thoughts about the opposite sex, and many of these thoughts or beliefs are confirmed by the media and other societal norms. How you were raised, where you went to school, where you worked previously, your friends, family, managers, ethnic background, cultures, and interests all play a part in creating your own stereotypical beliefs and personal biases.

The law concerning sexual harassment does not give you any guidance on how to fight or cope with personal values and feelings. It focuses on only the types of conduct or communications that are prohibited. However, you need to be in touch with some of your erroneous beliefs about sexual issues before you can begin to deal appropriately with sexual harassment. Recognizing and attempting to fight some of the more typical stereotypes and built-in biases will help you tremendously. Consider the following examples, which by no stretch of the imagination are all inclusive.

"Women Need to Be Protected"

Many men still feel that women need special protection in the workplace or elsewhere. This unjustified stereotype could have grave consequences for the male manager who attempts to remedy a complaint of sexual harassment. For example, a female subordinate may complain that one of the company's customers repeatedly makes sexually offensive comments and derogatory statements about women. You may feel compelled to remove the employee from the customer account to avoid any further inappropriate actions. Your stereotyped beliefs that women need to be protected will affect your judgment and make you think that this type of remedial action is the right thing to do.

In fact, your conduct in dealing with the situation could be construed as retaliation against the complaining female employee. Your need to offer "protection" may result in the female employee's losing a lucrative job or losing the respect or credibility she earned and deserved with the customer. Your paternalist and stereotypical beliefs will do nothing to correct the customer's unlawful behavior, and it could ultimately harm the complaining employee. You could also subject yourself and the company to legal liability because your conduct was influenced by stereotypical beliefs.

"This Is No Place for a Woman"

As arcane as this statement may sound, many men still believe that certain types of jobs should not be held by women. This stereotypical belief is perhaps most prevalent in the factory setting or construction trade jobs, but such stereotypes and biases are also expressed about women in white-collar jobs and senior management positions. You surely have heard about the glass ceiling that women can hit when they are trying to move up the organizational ladder.

Obviously, most, if not all, jobs can be performed by both men or women except in the rarest of circumstances. When members of one sex do not approve of a member of the opposite sex in their midst, they may feel justified in making that person feel uncomfortable and ultimately try to force the individual to quit. This can occur through sexually intimidating actions that range from subtle remarks to more blatant acts of hostile sexual behaviors. As a manager, you need to recognize that such stereotypes and actions still exist in the workplace despite all the hype about sexual harassment. Moreover, if *you* still believe there is any truth to this stereotype, you have your work cut out for you. Fighting the belief that "this is no place for a woman" is a must to deal properly with sexual harassment.

"Women Dress for Sexual Attention"

Believe it or not, some men still believe that a woman who wears tight clothing to work is seeking sexual attention. As a manager, you can probably do nothing to dispel this absurd notion, and hopefully you do not share this belief. Obviously, women wear tight clothing for a variety of reasons, not the least of which is that the woman may have gained weight. Equating tight clothing to a sexual invitation is a dangerous assumption and should be stopped in its tracks as soon as it is expressed.

Additionally, this stereotype may come up when someone is accused of sexual harassment and the person responds, "She asked for it." Never consider how a person dresses as evidence of consent to an individual's sexually harassing conduct. Consider only the conduct of the accused and how that conduct could be perceived.

"Everyone Plays Hard to Get"

Both men and women often act under the erroneous assumption that everyone plays hard to get when being asked out on a date or pursued for some sexual relationship. This general stereotypical thought may give someone mental license to persist in the pursuit. Clearly, this may or may not be the case, depending on the person being pursued. There may be no law against asking a coworker out on a date, but pursuing someone who has turned you down once or twice is coming dangerously close to sexual harassment and should always be avoided.

"Men Naturally Respond to a Woman in Distress"

Some men believe that a woman who smiles at them or asks for their help on the job has some personal interest or attraction to them independent of the working relationship. Women can have the same perceptions about a male coworker who is friendly to them. Again, as silly as this may sound, these stereotypes and biases are more prevalent than one would think.

Clearly, the fact that a woman may be friendly or ask for a man's assistance at the workplace may have absolutely no bearing on her feelings about that individual from a personal perspective. This can be a common area of misunderstanding for both sexes. Again, the point is never to assume anything and refrain from falling back on unjustified stereotypes that have no relevance in the working environment. Never think you are reading someone correctly based on actions or comments that could have several ambiguous meanings.

"Men Are Insecure and Need to Be Complimented"

Compliments, sincere or otherwise, pose a serious danger in terms of sexual harassment. It is also absurd to think that men are always insecure or that they need to be told how great they look. While it is perfectly appropriate to tell a man that he looks "nice," any comments about his sexuality, physique, or attractiveness should be avoided. Some men and women may be insecure and seek compliments. However, an equal number of men and women do not need any adoration from coworkers. The point is that it depends on the person, and you may not be the person from whom the individual wants any compliments.

"General Stereotypes Don't Hurt Anyone in Particular"

Many people truly believe that making a general negative comment that characterizes "all men" or "all women" in a certain way cannot be offensive because it is not directed to anyone in particular. This is perhaps one of the biggest fallacies when it comes to sexually harassing behavior. Make no mistake: the fact that general comments about a particular sex do not point to a specific individual can still be deemed hostile-environment sexual harassment. No gender-specific, derogatory, or stereotypical remarks, whether stated in jest or made with vitriolic force, belong in the workplace. If you or any employees make such comments, a sexual harassment complaint and possible lawsuit are almost certain to follow.

Handling Situations Beyond the Office Walls

Sexual harassment is not confined to the office. Even when you engage in other activities with coworkers, customers, vendors, or other individuals related to your organization, sexual harassment remains an issue. As a manager, you need to be aware of the more common situations where the extended workplace essentially becomes the workplace. In these situations, the standards of workplace behavior with respect to sexual harassment pertain. Never think that merely because you have left the office, sexual harassment cannot become an issue.

Company-Sponsored Events

Nearly all organizations have company-sponsored events such as parties, picnics, and other social activities. When these events are held off-site and liquor is served, they can become a fertile breeding ground for sexual harassment. Who hasn't witnessed the scene where an employee has had too much to drink and comes on strong to a coworker? Many managers ignore such behaviors because they may think it is "all in fun." These same managers would probably not allow such conduct to take place in the office. However, don't be fooled by the setting. Conduct that is unacceptable in the workplace is equally unacceptable at company-sponsored events.

Business Trips

Sexual harassment can occur on business trips. If you are traveling or attending out-of-town meetings with coworkers, your actions will be scrutinized in the same way as if you were sitting behind your desk. Business trips often involve late-night dinners and hotel stays. If late-night dinners are required, make sure you stay in the hotel dining room or some other restaurant, and never invite a coworker to your hotel room. If you do, you are asking for trouble.

Entertaining Customers or Vendors

Golf outings, dinner theaters, and the three-martini lunch may be good for business, but they are opportunities for sexual harassment to be alleged. When entertaining customers or vendors, liquor should be avoided and the entertainment choice should not lend itself to any questionable conduct. For example, avoid dark romantic restaurants, and limit physical contact to a professional handshake. Similarly, don't take a customer or vendor to the local strip club, as that could be equally inappropriate. Remember that you cannot judge the reactions or perceptions of your customers and vendors when they are being entertained. They may not object to your decision or conduct out of embarrassment or because they want to maintain a good business relationship, even if they are offended.

If you are advised of a client or customer who has engaged in some type of inappropriate sexual behavior against one of your employees during an entertainment event, take down all the facts and report it immediately to the designated person in your organization. Although your company's options may be limited when it comes to correcting the conduct of a nonemployee, you have a legal obligation to take a complaint, investigate, and engage in all reasonable efforts to correct the problem.

Socializing After Work

You may think that socializing after work is not part of the extended workplace because it is an informal or impromptu gathering and not a company-sponsored event. Don't be fooled. When you socialize with coworkers after office hours, your conduct is still under the microscope for purposes of sexual harassment. Even when your coworkers are your friends, sexual advances can still be unwelcome and inappropriate. Persistent attempts to put your arm around a coworker after a few drinks even though he or she protests should be a clear warning that your advances are unwelcome, whether or not you meant no harm. You risk being the accused in a sexual harassment complaint. The bottom line is that you can have fun and socialize with coworkers without crossing the sexual harassment line.

Understanding the Limits of the Corporate Culture

The corporate culture can have positive or negative effects on the way in which your organization deals with sexual harassment and implements its sexual harassment prevention policy. If the organization is committed to eradicating sexual harassment from the workplace and all managers have been educated about this commitment, the corporate culture can work to the organization's benefit. On the other hand, even when a policy is neatly in place, the corporate culture may be such that inappropriate behaviors are ignored in reality and management is not truly committed to understanding or preventing sexual harassment. The adverse effects of the corporate culture generally surface when employees insist on living by historical norms or when the company ignores the inappropriate conduct of productive employees or lucrative customers.

The "Always Been Like This" Mentality

Many organizations, particularly smaller ones or those with several small departments, may have a closely knit group of employees who not only work together but sometimes socialize together as well. The organization may be one in which social activities are encouraged outside the office, and sexual jokes, teasing, and other conduct with sexual overtones have been accepted by management. The attitude of employees in these organizations may be that sexual harassment is "no big deal" or overstated, and that "it has always been like this." Moreover, the fact that no employees have ever objected to inappropriate sexual behavior strengthens the myth that the conduct is appropriate.

Simply because employees may be friends who have historically tolerated questionable behavior and the fact that sexual harassment has been ignored does not mean that the corporate culture should continue. Sexual harassment is much too serious an offense to allow historical norms to control an organization's policy. It is never too late to say no. And remember, the fact that people may have tolerated certain conduct in the past does not mean that they approved of that conduct then or that they approve now.

Often people tolerate certain behaviors even when they do not approve until someone empowers them to speak up. The catalyst for this disapproval may be a new company policy on sexual harassment prevention, a training program highlighting the perils of inappropriate sexual conduct, or a manager who finally does the right thing and says, "Enough is enough." Whatever the reason, employees should not be held hostage by historical norms, particularly when those norms do not comply with the laws on sexual harassment.

Big Producers and the Customer as King

In some organizations, the corporate culture is to turn the other cheek when extremely productive employees or moneymaking customers engage in inappropriate conduct. Management may make excuses for the "big producer" employee with statements like, "He's just that way" or "He doesn't really mean anything by it." In turn, less productive employees may receive less deference by management. Clearly, the company's sexual harassment prevention policy and the law must apply equally to everyone. A top producer or a senior executive must be held to the same standard as a person in a more mundane or lower-producing job. Not only is the company violating the law by looking the other way when the big producer engages in sexual harassment, it also gives other employees the impression that management promotes favoritism and has a disingenuous attitude toward sexual harassment in the workplace.

Similarly, many organizations refrain from taking any action when a lucrative customer engages in inappropriate sexual behavior. Obviously, it is in the company's best interest to maintain a profitable relationship with its customers and clients. Thus, there may be a strong tendency not to confront the customer about his or her sexually harassing behaviors.

However, the "customer is king" mentality should never be promoted at the expense of employees. You need to balance your obligation to follow the law regarding sexual harassment with the need to keep a valued customer. Even when the customer is an especially lucrative one, ignoring an employee's complaint about a customer who repeatedly makes suggestive sexual remarks and sexual advances may ultimately cost the company tens of thousands of dollars in legal fees, with a good chance that the customer will be lost anyway. The point is that the company has an obligation to deal with the problem head-on and tactfully confront the customer about his or her conduct. A "so what?" attitude to protect big profits will do nothing but land you in court.

Promoting Respect, Dignity, and Professionalism

When assessing your own attitudes and conduct about sexual harassment, you must be cognizant of your own ability and obligation to treat every employee with respect, dignity, and professionalism. Employees must believe that you are serious about implementing the company's sexual harassment prevention policy without favoritism or bias against anyone who lodges a complaint. If you do not treat all employees equally while respecting their rights, it will be impossible for the company to gain the support and credibility it needs from all workers to deal with sexual harassment. As a manager, you need to be sensitive to the rights of others, or you will be perceived as ineffective in all of your management responsibilities.

When an issue or complaint about sexual harassment arises, you will not be seen as one who can adequately handle the problem.

Moreover, you need to assure employees that all inappropriate conduct will be dealt with promptly and appropriately. Petty, unprofessional, and irritating behavior creates an atmosphere of disregard for the individual, even if it does not rise to the level of sexual harassment in strict legal terms. If you allow such behavior to go unchecked or unpunished, you will be encouraging an atmosphere ripe for more serious conduct, which could rise to the level of sexual harassment. Thus, in order to be an effective manager when it comes to sexual harassment, you have to make every effort to convince employees that you will be responsive to their needs, keeping in mind that respect, dignity, and professionalism should guide your actions.

Handling Special Situations

Not every situation is addressed in the law, and many relationships in the workplace require careful thought, if not a creative mind, to ward off a potential sexual harassment complaint. Two of these special situations, the office romance and the "love-struck" subordinate, are of particular importance because under certain circumstances, they are sexual harassment cases waiting to happen.

The Office Romance

Title VII and the laws prohibiting sexual harassment do not prohibit an office romance. Obviously, this would be an intrusion on an individual's freedom of choice, if not the right to privacy. Consequently, employers are often in a quandary when it comes to office romances because of the possible ramifications. What happens if the romance goes sour? If the individuals have split on bad terms, a sexual harassment complaint may be inevitable. When one of the individuals brings a complaint, there is also the possibility that it may be false because of a strong ulterior motive. Nevertheless, the company still has a legal duty to take the complaint, conduct an investigation, and promptly implement remedial action, if necessary.

While it is unlikely that employers can completely end the practice of office romances, it is not unheard of to discourage the practice in a written policy or through verbal management directives. Make sure employees understand that although they have a right to date one another, they also have a right to turn down requests for a date. Employees should also be encouraged to request senior management's assistance when a romance goes sour in order to explore possible job changes to alleviate any tensions or bad feelings. For example, a worker may request a job transfer or a different shift. If the company is able to accommodate such a request, it should do so. However, be careful never to take such action automatically because it could be viewed as unlawful retaliation.

Regardless of the company's position on office romances in general, the best course of action is to discourage and avoid the situation of a manager dating a subordinate through a written policy or by verbal directives from senior management. Dating relationships must be truly consensual. When a manager is dating a subordinate, that issue becomes critical because a quid pro quo harassment case could be looming. In any event, keep your eyes open to any office romance that may be brewing and even discuss the situation with the individuals involved to head off possible problems. Tell the individuals that although the company cannot prohibit their relationship, they must maintain a certain decorum and autonomy in the workplace.

Finally, romantic alliances can create other problems in the workplace separate and apart from the issue of sexual harassment. If other employees perceive that an individual is being given preferential treatment because he or she is dating a supervisor, morale will suffer. Also, the company could suffer by the loss of a well-regarded employee if and when the parties end their relationship and one of the individuals decides to leave.

The "Love-Struck" Subordinate

What does a manager do when a subordinate engages in inappropriate conduct or makes sexual advances? The situation of the "love-struck" subordinate arises when an employee develops a crush and begins a course of conduct that is perhaps not illegal but clearly is inappropriate. For example, the manager may be showered with unsolicited comments about his appearance, talents, or management abilities. He may start receiving special gifts or notes that are not job related in any way. The more brazen love-struck employee may even suggest socializing after work, communicating by telephone after working hours, or going out on a date.

As in the case of the manager who dates a subordinate, the manager who encourages or ignores the love-struck subordinate is also skating on thin ice in the sexual harassment arena. At the first sign of any inappropriate conduct, you should immediately meet with the employee and explain that his or her actions cannot continue. You must be tactful yet firm, so that the employee will get the message that the conduct is not only inappropriate but unwelcome. Additionally, you should immediately report the incident to senior management officials who are responsible for investigating sexual harassment claims. In this way, senior management will already know about the background facts, and the employee's credibility will immediately be at issue if the subordinate employee becomes disenchanted because of rejection and files a sexual harassment complaint.

Twelve Important Questions to Ask When Monitoring Your Own Behavior

You need to assess whether you are in the habit of thinking or communicating in a sexual or negatively gender-specific manner, even though your intentions are not harmful. To avoid this problem, reflect on your own beliefs, attitudes, and behaviors, as well as your manner of communication. By understanding the issue of sexual harassment and recognizing that certain somewhat common behaviors may be inappropriate in the workplace, you will have an easier time of monitoring your own behavior and attempting to change inappropriate behaviors. The following twelve questions will help you with this task. If you check off any of the following boxes, you have some work to do.

- ❏ Do I kid around in a sexual way?
- ❏ Do I generally direct my humor to members of the opposite sex?
- ❏ Do I tell racy jokes no matter who is listening?
- ❏ Do I think members of the opposite sex are less able than I am?
- ❏ Do I frequently make remarks about how people look?

❑ Do I use obscene language when things go wrong?

❑ Do I use sexual language as part of my everyday conversation?

❑ Do I tend to touch people when I talk to them?

❑ Do I tend to make comments that are a put-down to one gender?

❑ Do I ignore the no's when asking someone for a date until I get a yes?

❑ Do I use sexual comments and gestures to intimidate people or gain power?

❑ Do I ignore conduct that I really think could be sexual harassment?

Answers to "Test Your Knowledge"

1. *Sexual harassment is in the eyes of a beholder. Anyone can label anything you do as sexual harassment.*

FALSE. Although each individual has a right to determine what he or she finds welcome or unwelcome regarding sexual advances, a person cannot categorize normal business communication such as a handshake, eye contact, or a meeting behind closed doors as inappropriate conduct or sexual harassment if no offending behavior of a sexual nature is present.

2. *If you are socializing with fellow managers who are your friends and you are all paying your own tab, you can tell sexual jokes and make sexual remarks.*

FALSE. Interaction with employees, regardless of the venue and whether the company or the individual is paying, must be free from sexual harassment. Meeting outside of work and paying out of your own pocket does not give you a license to violate company policy. Behaviors in off-site situations among coworkers can still be considered sexual harassment and be illegal.

3. *If someone has a complaint about your personal behavior, that person has an obligation to bring it to your attention and give you*

an opportunity to respond before bringing it to management's attention.

FALSE. No one is under an obligation to confront the alleged harasser unless he or she wishes to do so. However, if you are told directly by someone that your behavior is offensive, stop it immediately.

4. *If you have had a long-term consensual dating relationship with a coworker, it is not sexual harassment.*

TRUE. If the relationship is truly consensual, there is no sexual harassment. However, should the relationship end and you wish to rekindle it, be mindful of not harassing the other person with unwanted and inappropriate sexual advances.

5. *Giving someone the traditional pat on the back or the congratulatory hug is fine because it is not sexual in any way.*

FALSE. Touching, other than a handshake, is to be avoided. Physical contact, even when meant in the best of spirits, can be unwanted and perceived as sexual harassment in the eyes of the recipient.

6. *You should remove a female employee from any accounts where the client is known to be abusive and foul-mouthed, and thereby avoid potential sexual harassment suits.*

FALSE. This move may seem protective, but it can be extremely problematic and discriminatory. First, as soon as you are aware of the problem, the client needs to be informed that the abusive and foul language must stop, that it is contrary to company policy, and that it will not be tolerated in your organization. Second, protecting employees comes from addressing the source of the problem, not from "punishing" the victim or from "accommodating" sexually harassing behavior.

7. *A manager should avoid dating a subordinate.*

TRUE. Dating a subordinate is asking for trouble. The "consensual" nature of a dating relationship between unequals can be challenged by a subordinate who later decides that he or she was coerced into pleasing the boss. Claims of quid pro quo sexual harassment could result.

8. *A person can object to your behavior, but find the exact same behavior acceptable or even desirable from another person.*

TRUE. Personal preference, or simply whether you like a person, will often determine what you consider to be acceptable behavior from that person.

9. *It is impossible to know in absolute terms what everyone finds welcome or unwelcome; therefore, it is best to stay off sexually related topics in the workplace altogether.*

TRUE. Some people are quite overt about their feelings, constantly voicing their approval or disapproval. Others show their emotion in more subtle ways, such as through body language. Still others may have "poker faces" or show an emotion contrary to their true feelings. Therefore, rather than guessing, avoid these topics entirely so that you offend no one.

10. *"Locker-room" talk between the guys is okay if you confine it to the men's room.*

FALSE. All sensibilities are not neatly divided by gender. It is a sexist presumption that no man would find "locker-room" talk offensive. Be smart and avoid this type of conversation with all coworkers, anytime or anyplace.

Case Scenarios and Practical Guidance for the Real World

Scenario A

You manage the second shift at an automotive plant. Behavior by employees working on the assembly line has been fast and loose. There is no dress code, no close supervision, and no ban on sexual jokes or sexually graphic materials. Recently the company issued a sexual harassment prevention policy, and you told your team to clean up its act. The nude posters came down, but the sexual jokes and remarks are still flying. Everyone is now calling you a spoilsport.

Practical Guidance

You have a tough but not impossible job ahead of you. You need to change the historical culture of the environment while trying to preserve the fun and esprit de corps. Enlist everyone's support in understanding the effects of sexual harassment, and ask people whether they would approve of having their sexual jokes and gender-degrading comments directed at their sisters, spouses, mothers, or other loved ones. Help people understand that everyone has a right to be free of unwanted sexual advances. Show your wholehearted support by monitoring your own conduct and by treating all your employees with respect and dignity.

Scenario B

You manage a highly talented supervisor who is very cynical about the company's sexual harassment prevention policy. He is disruptive, claiming that most claims are frivolous and malicious. He also refuses to be alone with women in the office, insisting that his male assistant be included in every meeting.

Practical Guidance

First, you need to address the supervisor's attitude about sexual harassment head-on. Cynicism will do nothing but undermine the company's policy and impede the company's efforts to end sexual harassment in the eyes of the rest of the workforce. You must help educate this employee about why this is an important issue for the company and that the organization and all those in it must work to uphold the policy. Second, you need to counsel the supervisor about his refusal to be alone with members of the opposite sex. Not only is it impractical, it can amount to sex discrimination in its most basic form. Treating people differently because of their gender is against the law. The supervisor's conduct could cause women to be denied employment opportunities and access to information, and to suffer other adverse consequences.

Scenario C

You have a reputation at the office as a ladies' man. You relate well to women in a sexual way and are often flirtatious. Your conduct has served you well, and most women in the office find it to be flattering. Some even respond in kind. Recently you learned that one of the new secretaries is your daughter's best friend. You now become concerned about your reputation.

Practical Guidance

Consider yourself fortunate that you have the opportunity to assess your conduct on your own rather than as a result of a sexual harassment complaint. Start viewing the work environment as a strictly professional place and not a social event. Work to develop new habits to replace the old ones. Isolate your key vulnerabilities, such as touching, complimenting, kissing, staring, sexual innuendo, and the like. Replace such behavior with professional gestures and statements. Remember that you are in control of what you say and do. With practice, you can extinguish the behaviors from your repertoire that could lead to trouble.

Scenario D

You are on a business trip traveling with one of your managers. She has some of your files, and you ask her to bring them to your room. When she shows up, she is wearing a seductive dress and holding your files with a bottle of champagne.

Practical Guidance

Telling an employee to come to your hotel room is never a good idea. Rather, you need to have materials left for you at the front desk or send a bellhop to bring them to you. However, if you mistakenly created this situation, simply take the materials from the person without inviting her into your room. Any discussions should be outside your hotel room. If an extended conversation is necessary, suggest meeting for breakfast. In this situation, it may be presumptuous to assume that the dress and champagne are intended for you. However, if the employee indicates that they are, clearly decline the invitation, and plan to discuss the situation the next day when cooler heads prevail. The next day indicate that you made a mistake asking the employee to bring the materials to your room and that you want to correct what may have been a wrong impression. You should also report the incident to senior management for your own protection.

Scenario E

You reprimanded a new employee for using inappropriate sexual language when speaking with a coworker, who appeared uncomfortable with the comments. Your manager hears about the reprimand and doesn't support it. He tells you that the employee is "star material" and that you should back off.

Practical Guidance

Lack of managerial support is a serious issue and a breach of company policy in these circumstances. Report the situation to senior management. Permitting someone to disregard the policy because his or her talents are important sends the wrong message to everyone and undermines the entire sexual harassment prevention program.

Scenario F

You have recently completed a sexual harassment training program. You got the message out to the troops concerning what conduct is appropriate and inappropriate. Now you find yourself at dinner with a client and your new associate, fresh out of college. The client makes an obvious pass at your associate. The associate looks very embarrassed but remains silent.

Practical Guidance

This situation cannot go unaddressed. Either you can tell the client that this type of behavior is off-limits, or you can talk to the client privately after dinner and report the incident to senior management. You have a responsibility to speak up whenever you observe inappropriate behavior, whether it comes from an employee or a client.

Scenario G

You spent a lot of time and effort recruiting a woman who graduated first in her law school class. This morning you overheard her telling someone on the telephone that your firm is run like a "good old boys' club" and she wants out.

Practical Guidance

Your law firm's recruiting costs, training, and reputation as a desirable place to work are at risk. Open communications with this new employee about the specific things she has observed, heard about, or experienced at the firm that cause her to want to leave. Keep an open mind, and learn about the impressions that are being created. Take constructive steps to make changes, if appropriate. Your efforts can head off a sexual harassment complaint and help create the right workplace to foster everyone's development and success.

Scenario H

Your clients have always been entertained in strip clubs. It's an industry tradition. You asked your manager how this will be handled under the newly issued sexual harassment prevention policy and that you certainly put this type of entertainment in the "bad idea" category. Your manager says, "There's no pressure to take them to the clubs; take them anywhere you want. Just get the order." When you inform your clients about the change of entertainment venue, they start grumbling.

Practical Guidance

Supporting the sexual harassment policy and ensuring zero tolerance means eliminating both unlawful and inappropriate behaviors. In most circumstances, strip clubs and similar establishments are improper for entertaining clients, even though the clients may request them. All levels of management must support this message. Telling an employee to "just get the order" is not a constructive way to promote compliance. Rather, a manager should work with other managers to develop ideas for other appropriate entertainment venues and how to make it a positive change for the clients.

Scenario I

You are a midlevel male manager who supervises a department of mostly women. One of the women has been making what you consider to be sexual advances directed at you. She is quite attractive, and at first you were flattered and somewhat attracted to her, so you said nothing about it. Later, you decided that you were not interested. Further, she has made some openly suggestive remarks and gestures that have become a source of humor among the other women in the department. You told a fellow manager who is a friend about the situation, and he said you should enjoy the attention and stop complaining.

Practical Guidance

Even though you may have initially enjoyed or even encouraged the female employee by not speaking up, you eventually decided that you were not interested and that her sexual advances were unwanted. Although you should have stopped the employee's conduct immediately, it is never too late to say no. You have a right to be free of unwanted sexual advances even if they were welcome in the past, but are not welcome now. Tell the woman directly that her conduct is inappropriate and that it must stop. Then report the incident to senior management. The key point is to take action immediately. Be prepared to clarify when and how you communicated that the conduct was inappropriate and that the sexual advances were no longer welcome. Finally, do not heed your friend's advice.

Note

1. ___ U.S. ___, 118 S. Ct. 998 (1998).

CHAPTER 4

"Tell Me Your Troubles"
Taking In the Initial Complaint of Sexual Harassment

By now, there should be no confusion regarding an employer's legal obligation to implement prompt preventive and corrective action when it comes to sexual harassment. As the EEOC stated nearly twenty years ago, "An employer should take all steps necessary" to achieve this goal, which includes "informing employees of their right to raise and how to raise the issue of [sexual] harassment."[1] The focus of this chapter is to prepare managers for the expected and the unexpected when taking in an initial sexual harassment complaint. In many organizations, both large and small, the initial intake person is not necessarily part of the company's investigation team, which will ultimately gather all the facts and make recommendations for corrective action. In fact, many companies require that management representatives who first hear a sexual harassment complaint not take any action until senior management and those assigned to the investigation are notified.

Consequently, if you are hearing an employee's sexual harassment complaint for the first time, remember that you will set the tone for all the company's actions that follow. First impressions are lasting, and an employee's first impression of the company's sexual harassment policy will be formed when a complaint is made. If you appear to be insensitive or biased, the complaining employee, as well as the rest of the workforce who will undoubtedly hear about it, will form a negative first impression. The company's zero tolerance statement and the whole sexual harassment prevention policy will be undermined. If employees initially perceive the policy to be worth nothing more than the paper it is written on, management will never gain the credibility it needs to investigate and redress sexual harassment claims.

As the initial intake manager, you must try to get all the facts while remaining impartial and objective toward the employee's claims, no matter how frivolous or far-fetched they may seem. Remember that all sexual harassment complaints deserve equal and consistent treatment at this initial stage and until the investigation team begins a more in-depth look at the allegations. In Chapter 5, you will learn how the actual investigation should proceed, including a detailed discussion of witness interviewing techniques. Many of those techniques are also applicable to the initial intake and should be reviewed in conjunction with this chapter.

Test Your Knowledge

The duties and responsibilities of an initial intake manager for sexual harassment complaints are probably more complicated than you would think. Although they are based on good judgment and common sense, they involve more than simply listening to an employee's story and reporting to senior management or the investigation team. How do your skills rate? Answer the statements that follow, putting a T (for true) or an F (for false) before each one, and find out. Then read the rest of the chapter and compare your answers to those given at the end of the chapter.

True or False

_____ If a serious sexual harassment complaint is made, you should take immediate action to correct the problem based on good judgment and common sense.

_____ All employee complaints must be reported to senior management or the investigation team even if the facts being alleged clearly do not amount to sexual harassment or any violation of company policy.

_____ You should ignore a complaining employee's statement that "this complaint is not about sexual harassment" and nevertheless report it based on your own assessment of the facts.

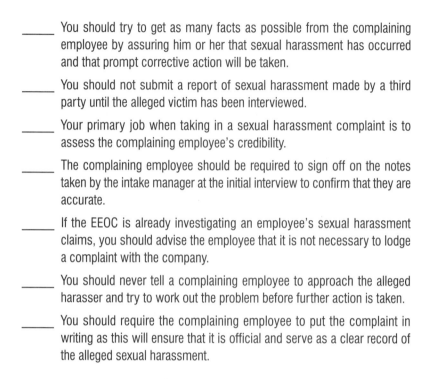

_____ You should try to get as many facts as possible from the complaining employee by assuring him or her that sexual harassment has occurred and that prompt corrective action will be taken.

_____ You should not submit a report of sexual harassment made by a third party until the alleged victim has been interviewed.

_____ Your primary job when taking in a sexual harassment complaint is to assess the complaining employee's credibility.

_____ The complaining employee should be required to sign off on the notes taken by the intake manager at the initial interview to confirm that they are accurate.

_____ If the EEOC is already investigating an employee's sexual harassment claims, you should advise the employee that it is not necessary to lodge a complaint with the company.

_____ You should never tell a complaining employee to approach the alleged harasser and try to work out the problem before further action is taken.

_____ You should require the complaining employee to put the complaint in writing as this will ensure that it is official and serve as a clear record of the alleged sexual harassment.

Recognizing Sexual Harassment Complaints

Every manager is responsible for recognizing sexual harassment and knowing when someone is lodging a complaint. This is true whether or not you have been designated as the initial contact person under the company's sexual harassment prevention policy. If you see obvious acts of sexual harassment, or more subtle ones, report them immediately, even if no one has complained. Your observations may amount to nothing, or they could be a catalyst for discovering something serious. The point is that all questionable conduct must be reported in furtherance of the company's zero tolerance policy and its legal obligation to prevent and take prompt remedial action against sexual harassment.

The "Direct Hit" Complaint

Sexual harassment can knock on a manager's door softly or with the force of a sledgehammer. It can also appear unannounced. The easy cases involve an employee who knows something about sexual harassment and gets right down to business, describing conduct that clearly fits the definition and accompanied by the statement, "I have been sexually harassed!" When you hear that an employee was demoted because he or she rebuffed a supervisor's request for sex, or that someone has been repeatedly subjected to lurid sexual comments, a sexual harassment alarm should ring in your ears louder than the Liberty Bell.

Also, never forget some of the basics of sexual harassment that may alert you to a possible complaint—for example:

- Sexual harassment is not always male against female or supervisor against subordinate.

- The victim or harasser can be of either sex. A male can sexually harass a male, and a female can sexually harass a female.

- The harasser does not have to be the victim's supervisor.

- The victim does not have to be the person to whom the sexual advances are directed. It can be an onlooker who finds the conduct sexually offensive.

- A sexual harassment complaint is not always against a coworker or manager. It can be lodged against a customer, vendor, or visitor to the company.

The "direct hit" cases are also the easiest to document. Employees who are somewhat familiar with their rights or have carefully read the company's sexual harassment prevention policy will already arrive in your office prepared. They will describe "who, what, where, when, and why" with little prompting. In these cases, your primary job is to fill in any of the gaps by asking follow-up questions so that a full picture of the event can be communicated to the investigation team. Even the less articulate complaining employee with a "direct hit" complaint should be easier to interview, providing you have done your homework and recognize that sexual harassment is at issue.

The "Murky Waters" Complaint

The harder cases are the ones where an employee is much less direct and the facts are murkier. Is it sexual harassment when a male employee complains that a female coworker comments that his haircut is "feminine looking"? Is it sexual harassment when a male employee repeatedly tells a male coworker that his "taste in women" is pathetic? Is it sexual harassment when employees constantly jar a fellow worker for having had an illicit extramarital affair? In all these examples, the employee may never use the words *sexual harassment*. He or she may even exclaim, "This isn't sexual harassment, but I think you should know about it."

In these cases you may have difficulty making a determination whether a sexual harassment complaint is really being made. However, always err on the side of safety. If an employee formally complains or simply makes a passing comment about conduct that could even be remotely considered sexually offensive, listen carefully, document it in writing, and immediately report it. Never allow any possible sexual harassment complaint to go unchecked. But at the same time, realize that it is not your responsibility to make a decision or pass judgment on the merits of any claim. All complaints have to be investigated thoroughly; only then will a determination be made as to whether sexual harassment in fact occurred. As the intake manager, your job is to obtain as much information as possible so that an effective investigation can proceed.

The "Knew or Should Have Known" Complaint

The "knew or should have known" complaint is really a misnomer because in these situations there are no employee complaints at all. However, a company can be held liable for sexual harassment even if no employee complains when the facts show that the company knew or should have known about sexually harassing conduct and nothing was done about it. You may recall from Chapter 1 that the U.S. Supreme Court recognized early on in *Meritor Savings Bank v. Vinson* that having a complaint procedure that was ignored by an employee may not get the company off the hook if the employer nevertheless had reason to know about the sexual harassment.[2]

Thus, you must be extremely perceptive and avoid a false sense of security about sexual harassment simply because no one has come forward with a complaint. The manager who knows of or suspects sexual harassment can never ignore it and assume that no one is offended or that sexual harassment did not take place because no one complained. Similarly, when sexual harassment is so obvious that a manager's head would have to be buried in the sand not to see it, the "I didn't know about it and nobody complained" excuse simply won't fly.

You have an obligation to report suspected incidents of sexual harassment even in the absence of an employee's coming forward. When you see employees engaging in lewd or offensive sexual conduct directed toward one or more coworkers, but none of the coworkers complains, never let it slide. Report it immediately to the investigation team. When you discover sexual graffiti on the lunchroom walls every morning yet no one complains, report it fast. When you hear through the grapevine that sexually explicit e-mails are appearing daily on the secretaries' computers, immediately report the incident.

Erring on the side of safety is essential. Report all suspected inappropriate sexual behaviors immediately. Never forget that the trigger for legal liability is sexual harassment itself and that the gun will go off whether or not someone complains.

Projecting the Right Image

Because the intake manager is an employee's first link to the company's sexual harassment prevention policy, it is critical to project the right image. This involves being aware of your actions and using common sense. In most situations, your comments, facial expressions, body language, listening skills, and general demeanor will be scrutinized by the complaining employee for several reasons. First, it is usually not easy to come forward and complain about something as personal and private as sex. Most employees will be uncomfortable or nervous. Thus, the complaining employee will initially assess whether you are truly concerned or simply going through the motions.

Second, a complaining employee will undoubtedly try to determine whether you are biased in any way. If there is a perception that you are not being objective or sincere, the employee will lose faith in any company policy touting zero tolerance and feel that making a complaint is futile. Finally, a complaining employee will try to obtain validation for the sexual harassment claims being made. The cardinal rule in this situation is never to tip your hand even if you think the events being described are tantamount to the most egregious case of sexual harassment on the face of the earth. It cannot be stressed enough that your only job is to get the facts and nothing more. Keep your thoughts, feelings, and opinions to yourself.

Listening With Both Ears

Listening skills are at the top of the list for projecting the right image. Having one ear glued to the telephone, signing company documents, conducting other business, or allowing any other distractions to undercut your listening abilities leaves the impression that the sexual harassment complaint is not being taken seriously. Carefully listen to everything the complaining employee says, and focus on the complaint being made. This means clearing your desk, holding your calls, and conducting the discussion in private. If your listening skills are impaired in any way, you will miss important facts and fail to conduct any necessary follow-up questioning that the investigation team needs to assess the claims.

Watching Your Demeanor

Managers often underestimate the effects of their general demeanor. Body language and facial expressions can say more to an employee than any words. Even if you personally think a sexual harassment complaint is completely bogus, never let your facial muscles form a scowl or a smirk and reveal what you really think. Crossed arms, crossed legs, or hands clasped behind the head should also be avoided. This type of body language can give an impression that you are hostile or uninterested in the allegations being made.

Consider your physical distance from the complaining employee when conducting an initial intake interview. Sitting behind a desk twenty feet away from the employee may create the perception that not only your body is miles away, but that your mind is also in some distant place. Pulling up a chair nearer to the employee is a much more effective way to show your interest and give the impression that you are taking the complaint seriously.

Setting the Procedural Stage

Both the initial intake manager and the investigator who first interview an alleged victim of sexual harassment must give certain assurances about how the company will handle the complaint in accordance with the company's sexual harassment prevention policy. This should be done at the start of the interview, before getting into all the details of the claim. These assurances are discussed in more detail in Chapter 5 under "Interviewer Disclosure Statement" and that section should be carefully reviewed, particularly if you are the manager designated to hear the initial sexual harassment complaint.

As intake manager, you need to explain three important factors with respect to filing a sexual harassment complaint:

1. The complaint will remain confidential to the greatest extent possible and will be disclosed only when necessary to follow up and correct any misconduct. This means that it may be disclosed to the alleged harasser, key witnesses, and those management officials with a need to know.

2. No retaliation will result from lodging a complaint of sexual harassment.

3. The company will follow its sexual harassment investigation procedures, including those for corrective action, and tell the complaining employee that he or she will be kept informed as the investigation proceeds.

Getting All the Facts and Writing Them Down

Good listening skills, body language, and saying the right things are all extremely important, but the manager who fails to get all the facts and write them down has fallen asleep on the job. A complaining employee may not be able to articulate all the facts of a sexual harassment claim, and you will most likely have to ask probing follow-up questions to make sure that all the facts, in chronological order, are disclosed. Specific, open-ended, and sometimes tough questioning is required. In addition to the basic facts, the relationship between the alleged victim and the alleged harasser, the names of any witnesses, and whether the conduct was unwelcome all need to be explored. Specific techniques and questions for interviewing the complaining employee are discussed in Chapter 5.

Memories alone are never a reliable record. Always write everything down, including what you said to the complaining employee. Strive for verbatim note-taking when possible. Remember that you will ultimately have to communicate with the investigation team about the complaint. If you get it wrong, they may too, and a faulty investigation will surely follow.

Finally, don't insist that the complaining employee sign off on your notes at the end of the initial intake meeting. Although you should ask for a signature, there is no legal requirement that this be done, and many employees feel intimidated or that the company is placing unreasonable burdens on the complaint procedure when asked to sign off at this stage. The investigation team will ultimately interview the complainant again, and a signature for the notes taken at that time will be more strongly encouraged.

Handling the Ten Most Difficult Complaining Employees

No two employees will ever describe the same event in exactly the same way. Some will be more forthcoming, discreet, or reluctant than others. Thus, as the initial intake manager, you will have to handle different complaining employees in different ways. Although the ultimate goal is to obtain as many facts as possible, you have to be flexible and know when to slow down or redirect the initial interviewing process. Following are specific ways to handle ten of the most difficult complaining employees.

The Upset or Angry Employee

It is only logical to assume that some employees will be upset or angry when making a complaint. You must make every attempt to calm such employees, without agreeing with any of their statements or acknowledging that sexual harassment has occurred. Never say, "Don't let it bother you," or "Nothing can be that serious," or "I am so sorry you had to go through that experience." Consoling an upset or angry employee is one thing; downplaying the seriousness of an offense or making apologies is quite another.

The savvy intake manager will politely tell the complaining employee, "Please remain calm, and try your best to tell me everything that has happened." Then state that the company encourages complaints, is committed to fighting sexual harassment, and will implement a complete investigation with appropriate corrective action. Build the employee's confidence and lessen anxieties with repeated assurances of company action, while remembering that you are a fact finder, and not a counselor.

The Shy, Inhibited, or Embarrassed Employee

The biggest challenge for the shy, inhibited, or embarrassed employee is approaching a manager in the first place, let alone raising the issue of sexual harassment. These employees will likely give a sketchy version of the facts and hesitate to elaborate. You should first tell the employee, "I understand how difficult this is, but we really need your help to understand what happened and to take whatever action may be necessary to correct it." These types of employees also need extra reassurance about confidentiality because that issue may be at the root of their concern about disclosing information. Firmly state that confidentiality will be respected and only those with a need to know will have access to the information discussed.

Finally, detailed and probing questions are a must for the shy, inhibited, or embarrassed employee. Ask the same question ten times in a slightly different manner if that is the only way you can get a straight answer. It may be difficult to get all the facts, and it may take more time than the typical intake interview. However, be careful never to show your frustration or impatience, and periodically reward the employee by expressing thanks for his or her cooperation in answering a question or disclosing certain facts.

The Uncooperative Employee

There will always be employees who come forward with allegations of sexual harassment, yet insist that the matter go no further or refuse to give all the facts and cooperate with an investigation. Regardless of the employee's reasons for not cooperating in the initial interview, never fall into the trap of failing to report the incident. A company has a duty to investigate all sexual harassment complaints.

Certainly you must be sensitive to the uncooperative employee's concerns, but the first order of business is to tell the employee that you are under a legal obligation to report the claims. Then stress the confidentiality aspects of any investigation and assure the employee that he or she will never suffer any reprisals as a result of the complaint. Additionally, ask why the employee is hesitating to disclose all the facts or refusing to cooperate, and then address the reasons given with firm, yet tactful answers.

For example, an employee may say, "I don't want my coworkers to know my business," or "I don't want the harasser to know that I'm the one who snitched." In these situations, you have to get the point across that preventing sexual harassment is a top priority for the company, and without the complaining employee's help, the accused could continue with the inappropriate conduct or harm someone else, and the whole workforce will suffer. This may border on putting the complaining employee on a guilt trip, but highlighting the broader picture often helps turn the tide for the uncooperative employee. Moreover, if the complaint involves an accused who is alleged to have committed offensive conduct against a group of employees, in some cases it may be possible to tell the complaining employee that his or her name will not have to be disclosed to the alleged harasser.

The uncooperative employee may also tell you that there is no need for the matter to go any further because he or she has filed a charge of discrimination with the EEOC or a grievance under a union contract. Regardless of these efforts, the company still has a duty to investigate the complaint promptly and take appropriate corrective action. Any EEOC or union grievance proceedings are totally independent from the company's legal obligations with respect to sexual harassment. In fact, management cannot let these simultaneous proceedings affect its investigation in any manner.

In *EEOC v. General Motors Corp.*, this principle was made clear.[3] There, management had a policy of suspending internal grievance procedures when an employee filed an EEOC charge or was pursuing some other administrative avenue of redress, independent of the company. Not only did the federal court rule that such a policy was unlawful under Title VII, it reasoned that a company engages in unlawful retaliation against a complaining employee if the complaint and investigation procedure is put on hold because the employee is pursuing other remedies.

The "Self-Help" Employee

There are two types of "self-help" employees. The first type confronts the alleged harasser and tells him or her to stop. If the sexual harassment does in fact end, no complaint is ever brought to management's attention and the matter is most likely resolved. The second type of "self-help" employee poses a greater challenge. Here, the employee has already confronted the alleged harasser, but the inappropriate conduct has not stopped. The complaining employee then lodges a complaint with management, but still insists on taking personal action to remedy the situation without waiting for management to take action.

This desire for more self-help often occurs when the complaining employee feels an obligation to report sexual harassment in accordance with the company's sexual harassment prevention policy, but may perceive that management will drag its feet with an investigation. Although employees are obviously entitled to make an attempt to redress sexual harassment by coworkers or supervisors on their own, once they have complained about the matter to management, self-help should be discouraged.

The self-help complaining employee may be in a hostile mood and tell you that he or she plans to confront the alleged perpetrator again with a stern warning to stop the conduct. Some employees may even threaten to recruit coworkers in an effort to confront and reprimand the harasser without waiting for management to act. In these cases, never encourage a "vigilante" effort or any other action that would further disrupt the workforce. Try to convince these complaining employees that their personal attempts have not worked and that now is the time for management to take over.

You also should tell the self-help employee that the company has invested considerable time and effort in educating its management staff on the perils of sexual harassment and that the investigation team is trained to begin an investigation immediately and report its findings, and that prompt corrective action will be taken if sexual harassment is found. In addition, the employee should be told that taking matters into his or her own hands may impede the investigation or create a more tenuous situation if the alleged harasser angrily reacts with additional offensive behavior toward the complaining employee or others.

The "Personal Relationship" Employee

What do you do when the complaining employee is a close friend or a relative? This can be a dilemma for several reasons. First, you have a duty to hear all complaints of sexual harassment no matter who is making the allegations. You cannot refuse to document and report a complaint simply because the complaining employee is a friend or relative and you may think you can informally resolve the matter. This is true even if the person raises the issue of sexual harassment outside the workplace. As difficult or awkward as it may be, as an intake manager, you must firmly state, "I will have to report this to the appropriate management officials."

Second, you have a duty to be impartial and objective. When you have a personal relationship with the complaining employee outside the workplace, it may be difficult to carry out these duties effectively. Additionally, the rest of the workforce may perceive that you are not up to the task. Impartiality and objectivity can become suspect regardless of your actions. In these situations, you have to be extra careful not to interject any of your own opinions or impressions. Even if you know that the alleged harasser is a "cad," keep your comments to yourself. Moreover, tell the complaining employee that you cannot give any personal reactions to the claims despite your personal relationship.

Finally, even if impartiality, objectivity, and restraint with respect to personal opinions can be maintained, you may still be tempted to forgo the investigation process and look for other ways to deal with the situation between friends. For example, your first reaction may be to delay any further reporting of the incident until confronting the alleged harasser with your friend, the complaining employee. Similarly, you may feel the need to talk to the alleged harasser alone in hopes of ending the sexual harassment without more formal action.

Three words of advice apply in both of the above scenarios: Never, never, never. You must never take matters into your own hands even when faced with pressure from the complaining employee. It is never the intake manager's job to redress claims of sexual harassment independently. All procedures must be followed consistently in every case, and you should never lose sight of your crucial role.

The "Credibility Problem" Employee

Inevitably you will be approached by an employee who has some serious credibility problem, which instinctively makes you think that the sexual harassment complaint is either completely false or has little merit. The "credibility problem" employee could raise suspicion for several reasons. The individual may be a chronic rule violator with several past disciplinary infractions or a poor performer. He or she may have a history of lying or engaging in some other conduct that would tarnish credibility. Finally, you may know that the employee has an ulterior motive that casts serious doubt on the validity of the sexual harassment complaint.

Once again, despite your suspicions or actual knowledge, you have no choice but to hear the complaint and take down all the facts as they are stated by the complaining employee. Never start with the presumption that someone is lying, or your job as the intake manager will never be fulfilled. However, when you know there are credibility problems, ask probing and specific questions, including detailed follow-up questions at every stage of the interview. Never disclose your doubts or appear biased in any way. Keep pressing the complaining employee for more details, and attempt to determine if your credibility fears are warranted.

Moreover, if you definitely know of a situation that would create an ulterior motive for bringing the complaint, focus on that issue without tipping your hand. For example, if you know that the employee was dating the coworker accused of sexual harassment and that the relationship recently went sour, focus on questions concerning the parties' history and the individual's reaction to the alleged sexual harassment. Ask whether the accused ever engaged in any unwelcome sexual conduct in the past, if the complaining employee ever engaged in the conduct now being complained of, or what the complaining employee said when the incident occurred. Hopefully, you will be able to detect whether the employee is being truthful or simply trying to get back at someone

Finally, keep in mind that you are not the judge and jury. You are simply there to record the facts and submit the complaint. Nevertheless, your knowledge about credibility problems and the complaining employee's demeanor should be communicated to those responsible for conducting the investigation so that they too will have all the facts, including those that you may be aware of.

The "Delayed Reaction" Employee

Victims of sexual harassment do not always report sexually offensive conduct immediately after it occurs. Embarrassment, attempts at self-help, or simply hoping that the sexual harassment will stop on its own are just some of the reasons that employees do not always come forward promptly. The "delayed reaction" employee is also more common when the alleged harasser is the employee's direct supervisor. Sometimes, the employee will quit a job, never having come forward with a sexual harassment complaint until he or she sues the company many months after separating from employment.

You may recall from Chapter 1 that this occurred in the recent U.S. Supreme Court case of *Faragher v. City of Boca Raton*, where Beth Ann Faragher was subjected to hostile-environment sexual harassment by her supervisors over several summers.[4] She did not complain until two months before she quit her job, and then only informally, and later sued for sexual harassment. Although the Supreme Court found that she did not act unreasonably because the City of Boca Raton had a faulty complaint procedure and sexual harassment prevention policy, the case illustrates how delays in reporting sexual harassment are quite common.

Regardless of the timing of an employee's complaint, management still has a duty to hear the complaint and promptly investigate. Whether two days, two months, or two years have passed, an employer's legal obligations with regard to the issue of sexual harassment do not fade with time. However, the time factor is not completely irrelevant. If someone unreasonably delays in reporting sexual harassment when an adequate prevention policy is in place, the fact that the delay occurred may help the company prove that the conduct was not unwelcome or that the complaining employee did not act reasonably in taking advantage of the preventive or corrective procedures offered by the company to handle sexual harassment complaints.

In other words, the "delayed reaction" employee may be the key to the company's successful defense of a sexual harassment lawsuit eventually filed by the employee. For example, in *Howard v. Burns Brothers, Inc.*, Mary Howard was an assistant manager at a gas station who alleged that a coworker often brushed up against her, "talked nasty," told jokes about women's breasts, and sexually harassed other female employees.[5] When another female employee alleged that she was harassed, Howard complained to her direct supervisor on the employee's behalf. Afterward, the supervisor refused to talk to her and would communicate with her only in writing.

Howard did not think the sexual harassment complaint was being handled properly, but she never reported her concerns to corporate management as permitted by the company's sexual harassment policy. Instead, she quit and sued the company, arguing that she had no choice but to quit because of the supervisor's conduct in handling the sexual harassment complaint.

A federal court in St. Louis ruled in favor of the company. The court acknowledged that the company had a sexual harassment policy that allowed employees to bypass direct supervisors and appeal complaints to management at corporate headquarters when they believed a claim had not been adequately resolved. In fact, the policy provided the names and telephone numbers of the individuals to contact. In the court's view, because Howard not only delayed but completely failed to utilize the company's sexual harassment policy and the remedies it provided, the company was not liable.

More recently, in *Montero v. AGCO Corp.*, Carrie Ann Montero worked in the company's business offices with two warehouse managers who she claimed repeatedly subjected her to sexually offensive verbal and physical behavior.[6] The company had a comprehensive sexual harassment prevention policy, which included a complaint procedure allowing an employee to bypass his or her supervisor to lodge a complaint. It also had a confidentiality provision. Although Montero complained about the harassment and the supervisors were disciplined, she waited two years before lodging the complaint. She later quit the company and sued for sexual harassment.

A federal court in California threw out the sexual harassment claims based on Montero's unreasonable two-year delay in reporting the incidents. She claimed that she knew about the employer's sexual harassment policy but feared that she would be retaliated against or that the company would not honor the policy and take action. The court rejected these claims, stating that there was no evidence to support them.

These cases illustrate the problems that a "delayed-reaction" employee may face if he or she ever decides to bring a legal action against the company. However, regardless of how the actions of the employee will eventually play out, you still have a duty to hear the initial complaint and obtain all the facts. If there has been a delay in reporting the incident, the investigation team will consider that as one factor when making its determination as to whether sexual harassment occurred.

Never tell the complaining employee that the claim is now futile because too much time has passed or "it's too late" for the company to engage in an investigation. Also, never express disapproval about the timeliness of the complaint or press the employee as to the reason for the delay. Simply asking the employee why he or she waited to report the incident is sufficient as part of the intake mission. But never insist on an answer or give the impression that the investigation will somehow be less thorough because of a delay in making the claim.

The "Helping Hand" Employee

The actual victim of sexual harassment is not always the person who comes forward to complain. Often a coworker will witness sexually harassing conduct, or the victim will disclose the facts to another employee. The company may find out about the sexual harassment only through these third parties, without any complaints from the person who was allegedly harassed. No matter who lodges the complaint or how the company finds out about sexual harassment, the duty to document and investigate the complaint never waivers. You must listen to a third party who is making a complaint, document all that is disclosed, and provide the same assurances about confidentiality, no retaliation, and the investigation process that would be made to an actual victim making a complaint.

Moreover, an employer must never require that only the victim can lodge a sexual harassment complaint in its policy or in practice. This principle was illustrated in a recent federal court case where a manager ignored claims from a victim's fiancé and was ultimately held liable for sexual harassment. In *Varner v. National Super Markets*, a grocery store had a sexual harassment policy directing employees who believed they were subjected to sexual harassment to contact certain managers in the human resources department or labor relations department.[7] The policy also provided that a supervisor who learned of a sexual harassment incident was to direct the employee to individuals in those departments and not take any action.

Over a period of several weeks, a fifty-one-year-old produce worker kept making graphic sexual comments and displaying pornographic pictures to a seventeen-year-old woman in the floral department. On one occasion, he sneaked up behind her and squeezed her breasts. When she went home that evening, she called her fiancé, who also worked for the store, and told him about it. The fiancé immediately called the store manager, but the store manager said there was nothing he could do unless the woman directly reported the incident to him. The store manager then said, "Just let it alone and maybe [the harasser] will leave her alone and forget about it." The woman never went directly to the store manager with her complaint, and consequently, the store manager never reported the incident to anyone.

A few months later, the harasser approached the woman again from behind, grabbed her breasts, and forced her hands behind her back near his crotch. The woman broke free and told a coworker what had happened. She also called her fiancé, who again called the store manager. The store manager made the same comments as before, saying that he could do nothing but that the woman could report the incident to someone in the human resources department.

The next day the woman had the harasser arrested. She subsequently sued the grocery store for sexual harassment and won. The store claimed it wasn't liable because the woman failed to use the sexual harassment complaint procedure. But the court quickly rejected that argument, ruling that her reports of the incidents through her fiancé were good enough. Once the store was on notice of possible sexual harassment, it had a legal obligation to investigate promptly and take corrective action. Because it was on notice yet did nothing, the company was held responsible.

The Confused Employee

In attempting to get the whole story from a complaining employee, you must try to elicit facts concerning whether the conduct being alleged was unwelcome and if the incident being described was actually sexual harassment. Although the safest course of action is to report any complaint, sometimes the employee's allegations are clearly not sexual harassment because they were not unwelcome or because the facts being disclosed do not even remotely amount to discrimination because of the employee's sex.

Remember that for an incident to be viewed as sexual harassment, the alleged victim must be subject to unwelcome sexual advances. If he or she invited the conduct or didn't perceive it to be sexually offensive, then it is not sexual harassment. In the real world, it is a rare case where an employee will come forward alleging lurid sexual conduct and then state, "I thought it was great, and it didn't offend me at all." However, you should never automatically presume that the conduct being described was unwelcome simply because the employee is coming forward. Nor should you presume that the conduct was welcome simply because it sounds as if the employee voluntarily submitted to certain sexual advances or other sexual conduct.

Probing questions on this issue are essential because it goes to the heart of an employer's initial defense. At some point in the interview, you must ask, "Did you find the conduct to be sexually offensive?" If the answer is no, explain to the employee that his or her observations are appreciated, but that the incident is probably not sexual harassment. However, the conduct being described may still be inappropriate and in violation of the company's zero tolerance policy. Thus, in appropriate circumstances, you should advise the complaining employee that the incident will be reported and dealt with accordingly.

Additionally, not every comment or discussion about sex in the workplace rises to the level of sexual harassment. As the Supreme Court recently stated in *Oncale v. Sundowner Offshore Services, Inc.*, Title VII is not some "general civility code for the American workplace," and "ordinary socializing" does not amount to sexual harassment.[8] Therefore, it is also fair game to ask employees why they believe the incident being described is sexual harassment. Sometimes an employee will think that anything said about sex is sexual harassment when in fact it is not.

For example, a male employee who complains that female employees in his department repeatedly discuss their pregnancies and childbirth experiences with graphic medical detail may find the discussion distasteful, but it is surely not evidence of sexual harassment. Similarly, hearing two employees discuss the scientific aspects of the sex lives of fruit flies after watching the Discovery Channel may turn off some coworkers, but it does not rise to the level of sexual harassment.

The point is that you need to use common sense and not jump to conclusions about sexual harassment before getting all the facts from the complaining employee. In clear-cut cases where the facts show that sexual harassment did not occur, it is appropriate to advise the complaining employee why further action is not warranted. However, if there is any sense that sexual harassment is even remotely at issue, immediately report the incident so that an investigation can proceed.

The Chronic Complainer

Every company has at least one chronic complainer—the employee who is always on the defensive, complains to management about anything and everything, and always perceives even the most innocuous comments from coworkers or managers to be offensive. This type of employee can also be the source of every sexual harassment complaint that has ever crossed a manager's desk. This employee regularly complains that someone has engaged in sexually offensive behavior directed at him or her personally or directed at someone else. The claims never have any merit after an investigation, yet they keep coming like clockwork.

Is there some point when an intake manager or senior management officials can tell the chronic complainer to stop making frivolous complaints? The answer to this question is a resounding no. Unless the complaints are unequivocally not sexual harassment, such as those given as examples in the previous section, the company is obligated to take the complaint and investigate promptly. Although the employee has an abysmal record of complaining, there is always the chance that there will be some validity to the allegations. Thus, be careful not to show bias based on the employee's track record of complaints and assess each complaint on its own merit. Anything less may put the company and your career at risk.

Checklist of Do's and Don'ts for Taking In a Sexual Harassment Complaint

The following checklist of Do's and Don'ts highlights the major responsibilities and the potential pitfalls of hearing the initial complaints of sexual harassment while putting the intake manager's job in perspective.

DO'S

☑ DO treat all sexual harassment complaints seriously.

☑ DO assume that the complainant believes he or she is telling the truth.

☑ DO show respect and sensitivity to the complainant even if you personally believe there is no merit to the claims.

☑ DO listen carefully.

☑ DO take accurate notes and document the full conversation, including the statements that you made to the complainant.

☑ DO allow the complainant to tell the full story.

☑ DO ask follow-up and probing questions to get as many facts as possible.

☑ DO give assurances of confidentiality on a need-to-know basis, no retaliation, and a commitment to keep the complainant advised of the progress of any investigation.

☑ DO ask the complainant if there is anything he or she believes should be done on an interim basis (e.g., job transfer, shift schedule changes) and that you will convey her request to senior management.

DON'TS

✗ DON'T fail to recognize a complaint of sexual harassment.

✗ DON'T promise absolute confidentiality.

✗ DON'T agree with the complainant that sexual harassment has occurred or disclose your own personal opinions, impressions, or feelings.

✗ DON'T ever ask questions about the employee's sex life, sexual history, or sexual proclivities.

✗ DON'T suggest that the complainant is being overly sensitive or taking the matter too seriously.

✗ DON'T make excuses for or defend the alleged perpetrator.

✗ DON'T delay in reporting the complaint to senior management or the investigation team.

✗ DON'T retaliate or give the impression of retaliation.

✗ DON'T criticize, debate, or argue with the complainant.

✗ DON'T suggest that the complainant should address the problem on his or her own.

✗ DON'T take any action on your own in terms of an investigation or remedial action unless you are given direct orders to do so.

Answers to "Test Your Knowledge"

1. *If a serious sexual harassment complaint is made, you should take immediate action to correct the problem based on good judgment and common sense.*

FALSE. The intake manager should immediately report all sexual harassment complaints, but never take any corrective action without being given authority to do so.

2. *All employee complaints must be reported to senior management or the investigation team even if the facts being alleged clearly do not amount to sexual harassment or any violation of company policy.*

FALSE. If the allegations clearly do not involve sexual harassment or other inappropriate conduct based on the company's sexual harassment prevention policy, the intake manager should advise the employee accordingly. However, if there is any remote possibility that sexual harassment has occurred, it should be reported. Erring on the side of safety and reporting all complaints, questionable or otherwise, is the best course of action.

3. *You should ignore a complaining employee's statement that "This complaint is not about sexual harassment" and nevertheless report it based on your own assessment of the facts.*

TRUE. The complaining employee's opinion about whether certain conduct is or is not sexual harassment should not control the manager's obligation to report the complaint and proceed with an investigation if the facts even remotely suggest that sexual harassment has occurred.

4. *You should try to get as many facts as possible from the complaining employee by assuring him or her that sexual harassment has occurred and that prompt corrective action will be taken.*

FALSE. Never use an opinion or assurance, justified or not, that sexual harassment has occurred to elicit more facts. Use only specific, detailed, and probing questions to get at the facts.

5. *You should not submit a report of sexual harassment made by a third party until the alleged victim has been interviewed.*

FALSE. A sexual harassment complaint made by a third party who either observed the incident or was told about it by the alleged victim must be reported. The fact that the alleged victim did not come forward is not controlling.

6. *Your primary job when taking in a sexual harassment complaint is to assess the complainant's credibility.*

FALSE. The intake manager's primary job is to obtain as many facts as possible from the person bringing the complaint. Although credibility is always considered, the investigation team will make a final assessment on that issue.

7. *The complaining employee should be required to sign off on the notes taken by the intake manager at the initial interview to confirm that they are accurate.*

FALSE. The intake manager cannot require the complaining employee to sign off on his or her notes of the interview. However, it can be suggested with a statement that the intake manager is simply trying to make sure that everything said and written down is accurate.

8. *If the EEOC is already investigating an employee's sexual harassment claims, you should advise the employee that it is not necessary to lodge a complaint with the company.*

FALSE. The company has a legal duty to hear sexual harassment complaints immediately, conduct a prompt investigation, and take swift corrective action. The fact that an employee may be pursuing administrative or other remedies has no bearing whatsoever on the company's legal obligations.

9. *You should never tell a complaining employee to approach the alleged harasser and try to work out the problem before further action is taken.*

TRUE. The time for self-help is before a complaint is brought to a manager's attention. A manager should never encourage self-help, but rather should tell the employee that the company will promptly investigate and take appropriate corrective action if sexual harassment is found.

10. *You should require the complaining employee to put the complaint in writing as this will ensure that it is official and serve as a clear record of the alleged sexual harassment.*
FALSE. You should never require that a sexual harassment complaint be made in writing because such a practice runs counter to a hassle-free complaint procedure, and it could have a chilling effect on an employee's willingness to come forward. Additionally, all sexual harassment complaints are official whether or not they are taken down in writing. The minute someone begins articulating events that involve sexually harassing conduct, there is an official complaint.

Case Scenarios and Practical Guidance for the Real World

Scenario A

A manager seeks your help. She believes a vice president who reports directly to you is sexually harassing her. You have worked with this vice president for a long time, and you consider him to be one of your closest friends at work.

Practical Guidance

Notwithstanding your friendship, you have just been put on notice about a sexual harassment complaint. Resist the temptation to take your friend aside and try to clear up the matter on your own informally. This is not the appropriate course of action, and it could seriously backfire, especially if the vice president denies the allegations or assures you that he will change his ways but does not. As a manager and agent of the company, the organization is legally on notice once someone in your capacity is told about a sexual harassment problem. Take the proper course of action: Listen to the employee, immediately report the incident, and encourage the woman manager to do the same. However, even if she chooses not to do so, the company still has a legal obligation to investigate the claims and take corrective action.

Scenario B

A very important customer makes a pass at a sales clerk you supervise, and the sales clerk comes to you for advice.

Practical Guidance

Your sexual harassment prevention policy should say that the organization has a responsibility to prevent sexual harassment from third parties, including customers, vendors, and visitors. How the situation is addressed and by whom will depend on the severity of the situation. You must report the complaint, and an investigation must be promptly initiated. If the investigation reveals that the customer did in fact sexually harass the clerk or behave in other offensive ways, someone in a position of authority at the company must speak with the customer, communicate the company's position on sexual harassment and zero tolerance policy, and instruct the customer to end the offensive conduct immediately.

Although your first instinct may be to remove an employee from an offensive situation, be careful not to "punish" or retaliate against the victim inadvertently by automatically directing a transfer. You could be setting yourself up for a retaliation charge because such actions can cause the employee to lose important responsibilities, income, or other benefits of the job. Discuss the matter with the employee before making any decisions in this regard.

Scenario C

Someone who used to work on your team, with whom you still maintain a friendly relationship, tells you in confidence that his new manager is flirting with him and constantly inviting him to dinner. The individual tells you he has no interest in pursuing anything but a professional relationship with the manager. He also says he doesn't want the matter to be pursued any further because he wants to stay on the good side of his new manager. Additionally, the new manager is a friend of yours.

Practical Guidance

Resist your instincts to become personally involved. At this stage you have a complaint that needs to be reported immediately. Explain to the employee that you are obligated by law to do this, and discuss his concerns about not wanting the matter to be pursued. Stress that there will be no reprisals for making a sexual harassment complaint and that the company strives to maintain confidentiality to the greatest extent possible. Avoid giving your opinion even though you are friendly with the employee, and tell him that you have a responsibility to remain neutral.

Scenario D

You have had a number of sexual harassment claims from employees who are marginal performers, and you think they are just looking for an excuse to avoid discipline or termination.

Practical Guidance

Part of being an effective manager means addressing performance problems as they occur and documenting efforts to correct the problem. Once a sexual harassment complaint is made and the employee is disciplined, he or she could allege that the discipline was in retaliation for lodging a complaint. Even if this is not true, the company will incur time, effort, and legal fees to defend itself. You need to be on special alert when discipline is imposed on someone who has complained and make sure you have legitimate reasons, independent of the sexual harassment claims. The fact that an employee may have an ulterior motive for making a claim will eventually be assessed by the investigation team and senior management when deciding whether sexual harassment actually occurred.

Notes

1. 29 C.F.R. sec. 1604.11 (f) (1980).
2. 477 U.S. 72 (1986).

3. 826 F. Supp. 1122 (N.D. Ill. 1993).
4. ___ U.S.___, 118 S. Ct. 2275 (1998).
5. 149 F.3d 835 (8th Cir. 1998).
6. 1998 U.S. Dist. Lexis 13956 (E.D. Ca. 1998).
7. 94 F.3d 1209 (8th Cir. 1996).
8. ___ U.S. ___, 118 S. Ct. 998 (1998).

CHAPTER 5

"Sherlock Holmes, Detective Clouseau, and Lieutenant Columbo All at Work"
Investigating Complaints of Sexual Harassment

The manner in which a company handles its investigation of a sexual harassment complaint is by far the most significant factor in determining whether it will be held liable for sexual harassment before a state or federal agency (e.g., the EEOC) or a court. If you are a manager responsible for handling these investigations at your company, you have important duties and responsibilities that you need to carry out with precision and objectivity. If you are not directly responsible for sexual harassment investigations, you still need to be acutely aware of the process in the event you receive a complaint of sexual harassment from one of your employees or you are accused yourself.

Sexual harassment investigations can be complex and tedious, or they can be quick and simple, depending on the nature of the complaint. Investigating an off-color sexual joke made by an employee in the lunchroom will be much less involved than investigating an accusation that the chief executive officer grabbed his assistant's breasts and propositioned her for sex on numerous occasions. But regardless of the nature of the complaint or the time necessary to complete an investigation, there is a process to follow in every case. To do otherwise will subject your company to potential legal liability, lower the morale of the workforce, give the impression of favoritism or bias, and ultimately put your own career on the line.

Speed, accuracy, objectivity, fairness, sensitivity, good faith, documentation, confidentiality, professionalism, and thoroughness are the touchstones for conducting a proper and effective investigation. These are high standards, but nothing less will do. In the light of the U.S. Supreme Court's decisions in *Ellerth* and *Faragher*, a company's defense to a hostile-environment sexual harassment claim is limited to proving that it exercised reasonable care to prevent and eliminate any sexual harassment and that the complaining employee unreasonably failed to take advantage of the company's policy and complaint procedures. Realistically, the only way to show that the company did in fact exercise reasonable care to prevent and, more significant, eliminate sexual harassment is to show that the investigation procedures were impeccable.

Test Your Knowledge

Trying to determine how to conduct an effective investigation from a single line in the employee handbook that "prompt investigations of all sexual harassment complaints will be made" is impossible. Whether your company has implemented detailed procedures or whether you must rely on the one-liner, the following test highlights some of the problem areas. Answer the statements now, putting a T (for true) or an F (for false) next to each one, read through this chapter, and compare your answers to the answers and explanations given at the end of this chapter. You may be surprised at what you already knew and what you learned.

True or False?

_____ **1.** Lawyers are the best people to handle sexual harassment complaints because they know the law and how to interview witnesses.

_____ **2.** An employee who alleges sexual harassment against his or her direct

_____ supervisor should be transferred to another department while the investigation is being conducted.

_____ **3.** An employer is under no legal obligation to continue a sexual harassment investigation if the complaining employee refuses to cooperate.

_____ **4.** An investigator should never review the personnel file of an accused harasser before an investigation begins because the information found could make the investigator biased.

_____ **5.** An investigator should tell a complaining employee during the initial interview whether his or her sexual harassment claim has any validity.

_____ **6.** Rumors and office gossip are sources of information that an investigator should consider.

_____ **7.** An employee complaining about sexual harassment should be required to sign a statement verifying that the investigator's interview notes are accurate.

_____ **8.** An investigator should allow the accused harasser to blow off steam about the allegations during an initial interview.

_____ **9.** A witness's body language is helpful in determining his or her credibility.

_____**10.** The primary goal of any sexual harassment investigation is to come to the "right" conclusion.

Choosing the Right Investigator

Before even considering how a sexual harassment investigation should proceed, a company needs to determine who will be in charge of it. This can be difficult because there are many choices, particularly in large organizations. In smaller companies the issue is often a foregone conclusion because there may be only a handful of managers to choose from, and budget constraints will limit any ability to widen the potential investigator pool. Nevertheless, every company should choose an investigator carefully, keeping in mind that the individual should have certain basic qualities and that there are only a limited number of choices.

"The Right Stuff": Basic Qualifications

The most important qualification for an investigator is that he or she must be impartial. Choosing someone who is the alleged victim's best friend or a potential witness to the sexual harassment being reported will surely raise a dark cloud over any attempts at impartiality. Therefore, if possible, a company using its own staff to conduct investigations should choose more than one manager as part of an investigation team. If any questions of impartiality then arise with respect to one of the team members, that individual can be excused, and there will be others to conduct the investigation. The investigation team should remain constant, perhaps being subject to an annual review, when new members can be chosen. In this way, the workforce is assured that any investigation into claims of sexual harassment will be handled consistently and without favoritism or bias.

In addition, an impartial investigator must be someone who is perceived to be, and in fact is, objective and fair. When the jury deliberates a sexual harassment case, they will follow the law, but their assessment of the facts will be affected by their perceptions of fairness. Did the company conduct its investigation in good faith? Was the investigator objective in reaching his or her conclusion? Was the investigation fundamentally fair based on everything that was done? If the jury answers any of these questions in the negative, the company will lose the case.

Moreover, an investigator has to be knowledgeable about basic investigation techniques and the law of sexual harassment. No one can conduct an adequate investigation on any issue without having some competent level of knowledge about the subject matter, the investigation process, and the legal implications. It is essential that an investigation team receive periodic training on sexual harassment, which includes some instruction on investigation techniques and legal developments.

Finally, anyone chosen to investigate a sexual harassment claim will most likely be required to testify if a case ever winds up in court. Because a jury will be most interested in how the company investigated a complaint, the investigator has the potential of being the company's star witness. Consequently, an individual's ability to convey the message that the investigation was conducted in a fair, objective, and reasonable manner must be considered. Someone with a negative disposition or who is overly shy or inarticulate may be a bad witness and could put the company's defense in jeopardy.

Choosing the Investigation Team

Keeping in mind that an investigator should possess the basic qualities just outlined, a company is usually limited to three choices for an investigation team—management staff, lawyers, and consultants— and there are pros and cons to each possible choice.

Management Staff

Most companies assign members of their management staff to handle sexual harassment investigations, for several reasons. First, it is less expensive than hiring lawyers or outside consultants. Second, a company with a personnel or human resources department may find that most managers in those departments have the basic skills to handle an investigation. Third, a company's management staff is already familiar with the organization and, in many cases, the employees involved in the sexual harassment complaint. Finally, there is more accountability when members of a company's own management staff are responsible for an investigation. If they handle this task inadequately, they will have to answer to upper management and suffer the consequences.

On the downside, investigations take time, and it may not be economically feasible for a company to tie up one or more of its managers for several days or weeks. This is particularly true in smaller organizations with a limited number of managers on staff. Additionally, the rank and file may perceive that an investigation by company managers will be partial. Finally, managers may feel burdened by and be resentful of the additional responsibilities, causing morale at the management level to suffer.

Lawyers

Deciding to use a lawyer to conduct a sexual harassment investigation, either in-house counsel or from an outside firm, has several advantages. First, lawyers are well versed on the law of sexual harassment and may lend more credibility to an investigation. Second, a lawyer will have experience in conducting investigations of this nature. Third, a lawyer, particularly one who is not employed by the company, will most likely be perceived as unbiased and objective. Finally, a lawyer may be well equipped to handle more serious sexual harassment complaints, such as those involving several employees or ones in which physical harassment is alleged.

Using lawyers is not without some negatives. Cost is a big factor to many companies, and everyone knows that lawyers do not come cheap. Additionally, many people are put off by lawyers, and a complaining employee, an alleged harasser, or a witness may feel intimidated and be less forthcoming with information. A lawyer who handles the investigation and gives advice to the company on how to proceed also may be compelled to testify in court about the advice given. Thus, the company may not be protected by the attorney-client privilege, which generally prevents the disclosure of a lawyer's legal advice. Finally, a lawyer who conducts the investigation cannot be the company's defense lawyer at a trial because he or she will have to be a witness on the company's behalf.

Consultants

Consultants professing to be experts on sexual harassment have proliferated as companies and the public at large have had to grapple with sexual harassment. Using a competent consultant to handle sexual harassment investigations often ensures impartiality, expertise on legal matters, tested investigation techniques, and a proved ability for giving witness testimony. On the other hand, consultants can be as expensive as, or cost even more than, lawyers, and it may be difficult to find a consultant who is truly everything he or she professes to be. Considerable time and effort will also have to be expended by a company's management staff to educate a consultant about the organization. Perhaps the best way to obtain a competent consultant is to ask for a referral from the company's lawyer. Many lawyers work with consultants and would welcome the opportunity to defend a sexual harassment case with the assistance of a consultant they know and trust.

The Investigator's Basic Duties and Responsibilities

The person ultimately chosen to be in charge of investigating a sexual harassment complaint has to establish that a reasonable, good-faith effort was made to determine whether sexual harassment actually occurred, regardless of the final outcome. In other words, even if the company's conclusions are later proved to be wrong in court, the fact that the investigation was properly handled may get the company off the hook.

This sort of investigation is hard work, and it has to be done fast. Moreover, the investigation is the most important aspect of any sexual harassment case. Not only do companies have a legal duty to investigate, but the courts and the EEOC have made it clear that companies better not drag their feet. And it should never be forgotten that a jury may ultimately decide whether an investigation was handled properly while it second-guesses a company's every move. Therefore, every investigator has certain basic duties and responsibilities to exercise in order to fulfill a company's legal obligation to take prompt action in response to a sexual harassment complaint.

Good Judgment Counts

The best investigators exercise good judgment from the outset to determine when an investigation is necessary. For example, the duty to investigate arises even when a complaining employee does not use the words *sexual harassment*. Thus, an investigator has to have good judgment from the start in order to determine if the allegations warrant further attention. This is not to suggest that minor complaints should be ignored, but a complaint from an employee that a coworker commented negatively on the color of her dress is surely not a sexual harassment complaint.

The duty to investigate also arises if a manager observes sexual harassment or inappropriate sexual conduct in the workplace, even when no one has formally complained. Thus, an investigator has to be acutely aware of what is going on in the workplace. Finally, the duty to investigate continues even when the alleged victim requests that no investigation be conducted or refuses to participate or cooperate in the investigation. Here, the investigator has a responsibility to inform the victim that the company has a legal obligation to investigate regardless of the victim's wishes, but that confidentiality will be maintained to the greatest possible extent.

Timeliness

Time is of the essence in any investigation because the law requires prompt remedial action for sexual harassment complaints. *Prompt* means "now," "today," or "immediately." It does not mean that a company can wait a few days until people return from vacation or until the management committee meets next week. In most cases, a sexual harassment investigation should begin as soon as the complaint is received, or at least within twenty-four hours. The time necessary to complete an investigation obviously depends on the seriousness of the allegations, the number of witnesses, and a slew of other factors. However, the "garden-variety" sexual harassment investigation should most likely be concluded within two or three days from when the complaint was received. Timely completion of the investigation will not be a problem if the complaint and investigation procedures are in place and institutionalized within the organization.

Confidentiality

Confidentiality should be at the forefront of an investigator's duties and responsibilities. Although a company cannot guarantee absolute confidentiality, alleged victims, alleged perpetrators, and witnesses must be assured from the outset that anything they say will be disclosed only to the extent necessary for conducting an adequate investigation. In addition to the complainant, the accused, and the investigation team, only management officials with a need to know should be privy to any information about the investigation. There is no need to disclose the details to other witnesses or to managers who have no stake in the outcome. For example, certain information may need to be disclosed to the victim's direct supervisor in order to make decisions regarding possible job accommodations. And the direct supervisor of the offender may need to be advised of the facts and take part in any decision regarding discipline. However, managers who have no involvement in the incident have no business knowing the details, and an investigator is well advised not to falter on the confidentiality issue.

Organizational Skills

Finally, no one can properly conduct an investigation of a sexual harassment complaint without being well organized. An investigator's organizational skills could very well make or break the outcome of a case if it eventually goes to court. An accurate and complete written record of the investigation needs to be carefully filed and maintained. This includes a written record of interviews with the alleged victim, the alleged perpetrator, and other witnesses. It also includes other evidence, such as documents, photographs, tape recordings, or any other items that may be uncovered. More important, after the investigation is completed, the investigator will need to document his or her findings in a written report, which will likely be reviewed by upper management or perhaps a court.

Without an organized, well-maintained investigation file, there will be an automatic presumption that the investigation was inadequate. Additionally, a poorly kept file will hinder the company's defense if an individual disciplined or fired for committing sexual harassment later sues the company for wrongful discharge, defamation, breach of contract, or a multitude of other possible claims. Finally, a well-organized investigation will validate the company's sexual harassment prevention policy by establishing that it takes complaints and the investigation process seriously.

Preinvestigation Checklist

Although the investigation itself is a weighty proposition, the preinvestigation process is equally important. Before you even start interviewing witnesses or gathering other evidence, review the following checklist to make sure that you understand your overall mission and that it can be accomplished with professionalism, expediency, fairness, and organization.

- Know when to investigate. Is it sexual harassment?

- Investigate regardless of the complainant's cooperation.

- Begin the investigation immediately (within twenty-four hours).

- Focus on objectivity and impartiality. Give no opinions or approval.

- Ensure confidentiality on a need-to-know basis.

- Recognize the objective: a reasonable, good-faith effort to decide.

- Get organized with labeled folders, checklists, and outlines.

- Write down everything said or done and maintain them in a file.

- Remember that you may be called as a company witness someday.

Primary Investigative Techniques for Witness Interviews

If you are assigned to investigate a sexual harassment complaint, or those who may be involved as one of the parties, you need to understand the primary investigative techniques for conducting witness interviews before an investigation actually begins. Interviewing witnesses is the most important aspect of any sexual harassment investigation. The complaining employee, the accused harasser, and any other witnesses will need to be interviewed promptly. No witnesses should be overlooked or ignored, no matter how minor a role they may have played. In fact, the federal courts have held that an employer engages in an insufficient sexual harassment investigation when only the complainant and the accused are interviewed.[1] Before embarking on any witness interview, however, you must take certain steps to ensure that this aspect of the investigation is well organized and properly implemented.

Initial Preparation

First, prepare a list of questions or an outline of areas to cover with each witness. This list or outline should be as detailed as possible based on the preliminary facts, gathered during the initial discussion with the complaining employee. However, it should serve merely as a checklist and not restrict the scope of an interview since new matters undoubtedly will be raised during the course of the interview. As the investigation proceeds, the witness outlines will need to be revised as new information is uncovered. There also may be a need to conduct multiple interviews of the same witness to gather all the important facts.

Second, review the personnel files and work history of each individual slated to be a witness. This information will enable you to determine whether the complaining employee has filed other complaints, whether the alleged harasser has ever been accused of similar conduct in the past, and whether any witness would have an ulterior motive or a reason to lie. For example, you may learn that the complainant was recently disciplined by the accused and was quite upset about it. Or you may discover that the accused had lied on an employment application or some other personnel document, which could cast doubt on his or her credibility.

This sort of information will help you prepare probing and detailed questions to elicit all the facts, but be very careful. Remember that your primary duty as investigator is to remain impartial. If information is uncovered before the interview that immediately puts in doubt a witness's credibility, you risk losing your impartiality and objectivity. Therefore, preliminary information about a witness that is derived from a personnel file or other source should be used only for the purpose of preparing adequate questions. Also, never assume automatically that the information is true. There are two sides to every story, and your only job is to make a good-faith effort to determine which side is more likely to be true.

Third, review the company's employment policies on sexual harassment and disciplinary procedures in general so that you have a complete understanding of the task at hand and the available options when the investigation concludes. It is also important to review these policies because they should be explained to each witness at the beginning of an interview so that the witness will have a clear picture of the procedures and possible outcomes.

Finally, consider how the interview will be conducted, including the timing and location of it. Common sense dictates that the interview should never be confrontational and that only you and the witness should be present. Additionally, the interview should be conducted at the workplace, during business hours, and in a private setting such as a conference room or your office. This should be standard practice unless the witness requests some other procedures based on the circumstances of a particular case.

Note Taking and Early Witness Assessments

An investigator must take detailed notes during a witness interview. This means taking down every word spoken by the witness. The goal is to record witness statements verbatim, if possible. Because this is an onerous task, many investigators prefer to use a tape recorder. However, never use such a device without first advising the witness and asking permission. Concealing a tape recording device is illegal in many states, and a sexual harassment investigation relying on "secret" tape recordings will never pass the "reasonable and fair" test. Explain to the witness that you are using the device only to make sure that your notes are accurate. If the witness feels uncomfortable having the conversation recorded or refuses to give permission, don't use a tape-recording device.

Witness interviews also need to be organized. A separate note pad should be used for each interview, with the name of the witness, the date, the time, and the place of the interview recorded at the top of the first page. If anyone other than the witness and the investigator is present, such as another manager to take notes, the names of those persons need to be recorded. The interview should be organized by following the outline of questions previously prepared. Start at the beginning, asking, "What is the first thing you observed and when?" A separate section of notes should be reserved for each witness to list any additional witnesses or other evidence that may be uncovered during the interview and will need to be pursued later.

Finally, never editorialize or draw premature conclusions when interviewing a witness. Your personal characterizations, opinions, or subjective assessments of the witness's statements should never be written down or disclosed to the witness during the actual interview. Notes in the margins like "sounds phony to me" or "probably lying" could haunt the company and you in the defense of a sexual harassment lawsuit. Your notes could end up in front of a jury and any off-hand written comments showing bias or lack of objectivity will surely taint the investigation. Any written record assessing a witness's credibility and demeanor should be made only in your final written report, after interviewing all witnesses and considering any other evidence.

Interviewer Disclosure Statement

Every witness interview should begin with the interviewer's making certain disclosures about the reason for the interview, the company's policy on sexual harassment, the investigation process, confidentiality, and no retaliation. The statement should advise the individual why the interview is taking place and that it is being done in compliance with the company's policy and legal duty to investigate sexual harassment complaints. The statement should then stress the seriousness of the investigation, the importance of obtaining accurate information, the confidentiality of the investigation and the consequences for not maintaining confidentiality (e.g., discipline), that only individuals with a need to know will be apprised of the information obtained in the investigation, and that no retaliation will occur for participating in the investigation.

Prepare this statement in writing beforehand and use it to begin each interview. Even reading the statement aloud is acceptable to make sure that the information is accurately conveyed. Afterward, ask the witness if he or she understands the statement and has any questions before the actual facts of the incident being investigated are discussed.

Specific, Open-Ended, and Tough Questioning

The investigator's ultimate goal during the interview process is to decide who is telling the truth, a difficult task because two or more versions of the same events are usually plausible. No one sees or hears anything in exactly the same way, and there will always be discrepancies among witnesses. Therefore, in order to assess the credibility of a witness, you must embark on a questioning strategy that elicits as much information as possible. There should be few limits on the type of questions asked, but keep in mind that you must maintain your professionalism and a sense of decorum during the interview.

Give a witness time to think about each question before answering, and never ask another question until you are sure the witness has completed an answer. Finally, get in the habit of occasionally recapping the witness's statements by repeating what you have been told and allowing the witness to confirm that you are accurately hearing and recording the information being disclosed. This process will also be comforting to the witness, because he or she will know that you are getting the full story.

Specific facts are needed from every witness, and the only way to get them is by asking specific questions with appropriate follow-up questions. For example, you may ask, "What time was it when Mr. Jones rubbed his shoulder against your breasts?" The witness may answer, "It was sometime in the morning." An ineffective investigator will leave it at that. A good investigator will follow up with, "Can you be more specific?" or "Was it before you took your coffee break or afterward?" The point is that the investigator has the ability to narrow down the possible times when the event could have occurred by asking specific questions with proper follow-up.

Ask open-ended questions whenever possible to require the witness to tell the whole story in his or her own words. For example, an initial question could be, "Tell me everything that happened that morning from the time you first came into work." After the witness has described the whole incident, you can then go back and ask more pointed questions on each aspect of the initial statement. This will undoubtedly lead to more information coming out and more questions to ask.

Avoid questions that require only a yes or no answer or leading questions. The worst thing an investigator can do is to assume facts or to ask questions that suggest the answer and require no elaboration—for example, "You saw Mrs. Smith in the lunchroom, right?" Even though the witness may in fact have seen Mrs. Smith in the lunchroom, the answer to the question will be a simple yes, and there may be more to the story, which the investigator will not hear. A good investigator will always ask, "Is there anything else you would like to tell me?" or "Is there anything else I should know?"

Additionally, part of your job as investigator when trying to get all the facts is to determine whether the witness is giving firsthand knowledge or is simply repeating office gossip, rumors, or a version of events heard from someone else. Determine only what the witness actually saw or heard. Rumors and gossip may lead to additional witnesses and other evidence that will require further investigation, but obtaining the firsthand knowledge of the witness being interviewed is the primary task.

Finally, as unpleasant and difficult as it may be, an investigator must sometimes ask tough and even embarrassing questions in order to ascertain the facts. Sexual harassment complaints can involve allegations of lurid and obscene sexual conduct, but all the graphic details need to come out. Shy or reserved witnesses pose the greatest challenge to an investigator dealing with alleged conduct that is sexually explicit. In these circumstances, display sensitivity and compassion, while recognizing that the answers to the questions may not come easy.

Ending the Interview

Never underestimate the importance of implementing proper closure to a witness interview. This involves much more than a simple, "Thank you for your time." After you have asked all the specific, probing, open-ended, tough, nonleading, and embarrassing questions, always ask one more time whether there is anything else that the witness would like to say or whether the witness can think of anything else that the investigator should know. Tell the witness to contact you if he or she thinks of anything after the interview has ended. It is also a good idea to ask the witness if there is any other person you should perhaps talk to.

In addition, tell the witness that there may be a need for a second interview after you have gathered additional evidence. This is very important because facts stated by one witness will inevitably be contested by another, and you will need to follow up with questions specifically related to such discrepancies. This will give the witness a chance to rebut any allegations or facts discovered later. Advising the witness of these follow-up procedures also conveys the message to all involved that the investigation is being conducted fairly, objectively, and without any bias.

Finally, the witness should read and review the written notes of the interview. Ask the witness if they are accurate, to make any needed revisions, and to sign and date the notes. This should be accomplished at the end of the interview before you and the witness part ways. However, if your notes are incomplete, sloppy, or unreadable, it may be necessary to have them typed and presented to the witness at a later date. But any delay could pose the risk that the witness will refuse to sign or change his or her story. Thus, the best approach is to obtain a signature on the spot.

The Ten Most Important Things an Investigator Needs to Know

A sexual harassment investigation involves more than the typical who, what, where, when, and why. Although such basic facts are important, an investigator needs to know much more in order to conduct an effective investigation when the issue is sexual harassment. The following list highlights the ten most important things an investigator needs to know:

1. The identity of the alleged harasser

2. How the incident occurred (e.g., what the individuals were doing or what was being talked about when the alleged sexual harassment took place)

3. Precisely what was said and done by each individual, as if describing a scene in a movie

4. Whether the incident was isolated or part of a pattern or practice of conduct

5. How the complainant reacted to the accused and how the accused reacted to the complainant, both at the time of the incident and afterward

6. The effect of the incident on the complainant, both at the time of the incident and afterward

7. All witnesses to the incident

8. Whether the complainant or the accused has spoken to anyone else about the incident, even noncoworkers, and the details of those conversations

9. Whether there is any documentation or physical evidence of the incident, such as calendars, diaries, notes, photos, or recordings

10. Whether any witness is aware of other individuals who have been subjected to unwanted sexual conduct at the workplace

Interviewing the Complainant

The most important witness in any sexual harassment case is the complainant. Explaining the investigation procedures, encouraging cooperation, giving assurances about confidentiality and against retaliatory actions, asking specific questions, attempting to elicit every fact and thought in the complainant's mind, and utilizing "the ten most important things" checklist are all essential to conducting an effective interview. However, additional important factors need to be considered when interviewing the complainant. The complainant's interview can set the tone for the entire investigation and lead to additional witnesses and evidence. If it is handled improperly, the whole process will suffer. As such, the following elements should be part of any complainant interview:

1. Ask if the complainant is comfortable with you as the investigator and whether he or she believes that you can be impartial. If the complainant has any hesitation, someone else may need to

be the investigator. Otherwise, it will be difficult to obtain the complainant's full cooperation and truthfulness.

2. Establish the reporting relationship, if any, between the complainant and the accused. Is the complainant alleging sexual harassment by a direct supervisor, a manager in another department, a coworker, or a visitor to the company? An allegation that a direct supervisor or some other manager with decision-making power over the terms and conditions of the complainant's job should be given more serious attention; if in fact some penalty or benefit was given, the company may have no defense to a sexual harassment lawsuit.

3. Determine the exact nature of the relationship between the complainant and the accused immediately prior to the alleged incident. Were they friends? Did they socialize outside the office? Was there some romantic involvement? Did the complainant give the accused gifts or cards, make personal telephone calls to the accused, or send him or her e-mails and facsimiles? Did the complainant make any other overtures of a personal nature? Such inquiries can be extremely important when assessing credibility and the issue of unwelcome sexual conduct. You also need to ask these types of questions in order to determine whether there may be some ulterior motive for the sexual harassment complaint (e.g., jilted lover, personal disagreement).

4. In addition to being detail oriented with questions, don't accept the complainant's conclusions such as, "It was harassment." Ask why the complainant believes this to be true. Also, ask if the complainant found the conduct to be offensive and why. Did he or she communicate in any way to the accused that the conduct was unwelcome, and did the accused respond in any way?

5. Determine whether the complainant has previously lodged a sexual harassment complaint, whether it was against the same person, and the outcome. This information may shed light on the complainant's motives or raise a red flag that someone at the company has propensities for sexually harassing conduct that need immediate attention.

6. Ask how the alleged incident affected the complainant in terms of any adverse consequences or harm suffered (e.g., monetary losses, job penalties or benefits, medical expenses). You will need this information to assess possible damages or for deciding the appropriate corrective action.

7. Ask whether the complainant needs any type of an accommodation in the light of the alleged sexual harassment—for example, a job transfer, a leave of absence, a job or shift reassignment, or a change in supervision for either the complainant or the accused. The goal here is to minimize interpersonal conflicts during and after the investigation. Therefore, these options can be considered at any time, depending on the circumstances of the case. However, any investigator has to be extremely cautious when dealing with the accommodation issue because there must not be any appearance of retaliation against the complainant. Never take any action without first asking the complainant if he or she feels it is necessary.

8. Be prepared for questions about how the investigation will proceed. The complainant should be informed that the accused will be interviewed and told about the allegations. The complainant should also be reassured again that confidentiality will be maintained to the greatest extent possible without impeding the investigation.

9. Be prepared for inquiries about your opinion, impression, or judgment about the validity of the complainant's allegations. All too often complainants ask the investigator questions such as, "What do you think?" or "Isn't this the worst case you have ever seen!" or "This guy is going to be fired, isn't he?" Never, never, never offer an opinion or respond to such questions. Instead, explain that the allegations will need to be considered after all the evidence is collected and that any conclusions would be premature at this time.

10. Be prepared for the uncooperative complainant. Sometimes a complainant will withhold names and details, phrase allegations in broad, general ways without responding to specific questions, or refuse to cooperate in other ways. In these situations, proceed nonetheless by gathering whatever information

is available from other sources. More important, the complainant must be told that the investigation will proceed and that the company will make a determination concerning the alleged sexual harassment based on other evidence, as well as any inferences drawn from the complainant's refusal to cooperate.

Make a written record of the complainant's refusal to cooperate for the investigation file. The document should state the ways in which the complainant would not cooperate and reiterate the assurances given to the complainant (e.g., need for cooperation, encouragement to come forward, confidentiality). Such a document will be invaluable if a lawsuit is ever filed and the complainant argues that the company failed to conduct a proper investigation.

11. Be prepared for the complainant who wants a lawyer or a coworker present during the interview. In a union organization, an employer may have a legal obligation to grant an employee's request for representation, albeit not necessarily a lawyer, during an investigatory interview that an employee reasonably believes might eventually result in disciplinary action.[2] Even though it is unlikely that the complainant will be disciplined, a company should probably allow a complainant who is a union worker to have a representative present upon request. In the nonunion setting, there is no parallel legal requirement. However, if the complainant requests that his or her attorney be present, you should try to discourage it. Explain that the interviewing process is not meant to be an adversarial proceeding and that the goal is merely to try to get all the facts. If the complainant insists, you should allow the attorney to be present. Remember that the company may have to defend itself later in court, and telling a jury that the investigator refused to allow a complainant to have legal representation may smack of unfairness in the jury's mind. If legal representation is permitted for the complainant, it is probably a good idea to have a company lawyer present. Even though this may unfortunately turn the investigation into an adversarial proceeding, the company's legal interests need to be protected.

Interviewing the Accused

Generally the accused should be interviewed immediately after the complainant, although sometimes the investigator will want to obtain background information from other witnesses first. This strategy could apply when the accused has been involved in previous allegations of sexual harassment or when multiple incidents involving several victims are reported and as investigator you need to meet with other third-party witnesses before interviewing the alleged harasser.

The issue of legal representation is likely to come up again when arranging to interview the accused. Allegations of sexual harassment are serious, and the accused may not cooperate without having a lawyer present. There also may be circumstances where a criminal assault case or other legal proceedings are pending that relate to the sexual harassment claims. Consequently, legal representation for the accused should be allowed, but a company lawyer should also be present. Additionally, always remember that the company's duty to investigate continues regardless of other legal or administrative actions based on the sexual harassment complaint.

The interview of the accused should begin with your disclosure statements concerning confidentiality, cooperation, fairness, and the way in which the entire investigation will be conducted. It is also important to stress the company's zero tolerance policy to impress on the accused that no inappropriate sexual behavior will be tolerated. The accused must realize at the outset of the interview that all allegations of sexual harassment are taken very seriously by the company even if they ultimately prove to be false. Explain that the interview should not be confrontational, that you are making no judgments, and that you are merely doing your job.

Interviewing the accused is probably the investigator's hardest job. There will, no doubt, be anger, frustration, and resentment on the part of the accused, whether or not sexual harassment has actually occurred. Therefore, you must remain calm and be careful not to suggest any bias with commentary or body language. Several other important factors should be part of the interview:

1. Explain all the allegations of sexual harassment made by the complainant. This means providing the accused with all the

details, regardless of how sexually graphic or embarrassing they may be. The accused must be given the opportunity to respond to everything alleged, and you cannot miss anything in this regard.

2. If the accused flatly denies all or part of the allegations, ask what he or she thinks would motivate the complainant to lie or to misrepresent or conceal facts. This is an important question because the complainant may not have been forthcoming with accurate information regarding the history of the parties' relationship or the actual events. Therefore, be sure to refer to the notes taken during the complainant's interview, and follow up with the accused by asking probing questions regarding every detail.

3. If the accused claims that the complainant welcomed or invited the conduct, ask for detailed supporting facts (e.g., conduct engaged in by complainant, dates, witnesses, context, statements), and never let self-serving statements such as "He was asking for it" or "She always came on to me" go unchecked. Always follow up with probing questions, while making sure that the accused is given every opportunity to rebut every allegation.

4. Tell the accused that absolutely no reprisals can be taken against the complainant, and carefully explain the legal ramifications of retaliation. In most cases, the accused should be told to stay away from the complainant, make no contact, and have no communications whatsoever. Additionally, stress that any violation of these instructions, or any evidence of retaliatory conduct by the accused, could result in discipline up to and including discharge, independent of any discipline that may be imposed if sexual harassment is found.

5. Anticipate concealment by the accused due to embarrassment or privacy concerns. Again, stress the confidential nature of the investigation in an attempt to bring out the facts. Tell the accused that concealing any of the facts will only make the situation worse and could lead to the wrong conclusion.

6. Be extremely careful not to turn the interview into an investigation of the possible victim rather than the accused. Irrelevant,

derogatory comments about the complainant should not be tolerated. And never allow the accused to get off the track by raising issues about the complainant that are in no way related to the sexual harassment complaint.

Interviewing Other Witnesses

All persons with knowledge of the facts, including any witnesses identified by either the complainant or the accused, should be interviewed promptly. These interviews should be conducted individually, with the same assurances of confidentiality and against retaliation that were given to the primary parties. Again, advise the witnesses of the company's legal responsibility to investigate sexual harassment complaints promptly and that full cooperation and truthful answers are needed from everyone involved to ensure that the matter is handled and resolved properly.

Be careful when disclosing the subject matter of the sexual harassment complaint to third-party witnesses. Obviously the witness must be told why he or she is being interviewed and that a sexual harassment complaint has been lodged. However, it is not always necessary, or advisable, to tell the witness every detail of the complaint. In keeping with the commitment to preserve confidentiality whenever possible, a third-party witness should be told of only those facts that pertain to him or her. For example, if you have been told that the witness was present only during an alleged incident in the company parking lot, there is no reason to disclose that part of the allegations involved sexual harassing behavior in the company lunchroom, where the witness was not present.

Ask detailed, probing questions, and obtain each witness's complete version of events. It is very important to make sure that the witness has firsthand knowledge and is not simply talking about the alleged harassment in some abstract sense. What did the witness actually see and hear? Who initiated the alleged conduct? What is known about the relationship between the complainant and the accused? What has been observed since the incident occurred? These and many other questions are needed to get the whole picture and to help assess the credibility of the complainant and the accused.

Conclude the interview with a firm statement that the witness should not discuss anything about the interview with anyone. Unfortunately, third-party witnesses are often the source of office gossip and rumors. Convey the message that sexual harassment is a serious and sensitive subject, and that a breach of confidentiality will not be tolerated and could result in discipline.

Reinterviewing the Complainant, the Accused, and Other Witnesses

In most cases it is necessary to reinterview the complainant and the accused after all witnesses have been initially interviewed. No investigation is complete without obtaining the complainant's reaction and statements to the alleged harasser's side of the story. No investigation will ever be clear-cut except in the rare case when the accused admits that the sexual harassment did take place as described by the complainant. Usually it will not be necessary to reinterview third-party witnesses unless new information is raised or there is a need to clarify some earlier statement.

The interviewing stage of the investigation should conclude with a final interview of the alleged harasser, especially in a serious or complicated case. Although a sexual harassment investigation is not a criminal trial, the old adage that someone is innocent until proved guilty should be followed. The accused needs to be given every opportunity to offer a response and rebuttal to every allegation. Anything less will give the appearance of a witch-hunt and fairness will be compromised.

Obtaining Other Evidence

Aside from interviews, it may be necessary for the investigation to include an examination of documents or other evidence referred to in a witness interview. As investigator, you must consider all possible evidence in an effort to corroborate a fact reported by a witness. For example, if an alleged victim claims that a coemployee brushed up against her while passing through a certain work area and the coemployee admits the physical conduct but claims that it was unavoidable because the work area was small, the investigator should take a tour of the work area to assess whether that contact was truly unavoidable due to space constraints. Essentially, the investigator should do whatever is necessary to uncover the truth as to what occurred.

Whom to Believe?

After all the witnesses have been interviewed and the other evidence reviewed, you must reach a conclusion about what actually happened. This is not a criminal trial, and it is not necessary for the alleged victim to have proved his or her version of events beyond a reasonable doubt. In arriving at a conclusion, however, consider whether the facts given by a particular witness are based on first-hand knowledge or merely office gossip. Also review each party's reputation, motivations, demeanor when being interviewed, and history of complaints.

In most instances, the alleged victim will make certain claims that the accused will deny. You as the investigator will then have the frustrating task of determining who is telling the truth. In dealing with the she said/he said dilemma, the following factors may help you make a determination about the credibility or lack of trustworthiness of a witness:

- The witness's demeanor during the interview (e.g., blushing, nervous gestures, irregular speech patterns, fidgeting)

- Failure to make eye contact during interview

- Blanket denials and/or short, clipped denials

- Motives to lie (e.g., the alleged victim's trying to get revenge on harasser; the victim's using a claim to effectuate a change in employment denied earlier by company; an alleged harasser on probation for other performance problems at the time of allegation who recognizes that admission of behavior will result in his or her termination)

- Changing story when confronted with conflicting evidence from other sources

- Catching the individual in a lie or a proved history of lying

- Stating facts that you know cannot be true

- The accuracy of the witness's account measured against other facts

- Inconsistencies in the witness's own story, particularly after a second interview when rebuttals or new information has been presented

As the investigator, do not hesitate to make credibility findings in reaching a conclusion as to what happened. However, don't base your credibility findings on anything but the facts. In other words, don't report things like, "She acted a little weird when I interviewed her and I think she's lying." A correct statement would be, "She kept twitching and looking away from me during the interview, and her story kept changing when I asked her how the incident occurred." In this way, you are making a good-faith effort to base your credibility conclusions on actual facts, not on some general observation or impression.

Investigator Don'ts: The Twelve Most Common Mistakes

Even the most sophisticated investigator can be caught off guard by his or her own biases and perceptions when conducting witness interviews and attempting to assess the facts of a given case. A "gut reaction" or just plain "instinct" can slip through the shield of impartiality, causing you to lose credibility and possibly resulting in a tainted conclusion. Here is how you can avoid making the twelve most common mistakes of investigators during the investigation of a sexual harassment complaint:

- ✗ DON'T tell the complainant not to let the offensive conduct bother him or her.

- ✗ DON'T tell the complainant that dealing with the complaint may cause embarrassment, hurt his or her career or reputation, or cause harm and embarrassment to someone else.

- ✗ DON'T tell a female complainant that she should expect this kind of behavior from a workforce consisting primarily of men.

✘ DON'T tell a female complainant that she might have mis-understood what the accused harasser intended.

✘ DON'T tell the complainant that the accused harasser "is just like that sometimes," or "just a joker," or "doesn't really mean anything by it."

✘ DON'T discount the credibility of the complainant simply because he or she has had disciplinary problems or has made unsubstantiated complaints of sexual harassment in the past.

✘ DON'T discount the credibility of the complainant because he or she is known to be sexually provocative, promiscuous, or flirtatious with coworkers.

✘ DON'T discount the credibility of the complainant because of a delay in reporting the incident.

✘ DON'T fail to follow up with probing interviews of the wit-nesses mentioned by both the complainant and the accused harasser.

✘ DON'T tell the accused harasser to stay away from or avoid the complainant as a substitute for investigating whether the alleged acts occurred.

✘ DON'T tell the complainant that the alleged facts are "awful," or that the accused harasser "should never have done any-thing like that" or "has done things like that before."

✘ DON'T fail to keep both the complainant and the accused harasser advised that the investigation is in process and that they will be notified of the results when completed.

Documenting Your Findings, Conclusions, and Recommendations in a Final Report

Everyone has heard of the three rules of real estate: "location, loca-tion, location." There are also three rules for sexual harassment investigations: "documentation, documentation, documentation." You should have written down everything during the course of your investigation, and now that the investigation is complete, you must consolidate all your materials into an organized, easy-to-understand report with conclusions and recommendations. Avoid being subjective. State the facts you found, and draw a conclusion without unfounded opinions or editorials. The following outline is a suggested guide for the report:

1. A statement of the actual complaint, including all persons alleged to be involved.

2. A separate statement for each witness interviewed and the details of their stories.

3. A statement containing any rebuttal or new facts disclosed from second interviews with the alleged victim and harasser.

4. A statement listing all the other evidence you obtained, including your sources. If there are documents, attach them to your report.

5. A statement of your conclusions answering the ultimate question of whether the conduct alleged was likely to have occurred based on the facts you uncovered. Do not say what you think, feel, or believe. Rather, state that "based on these facts, I conclude the following . . . ."

6. A statement of your recommended actions. You have one of two choices here: No inappropriate conduct occurred, or it did occur and you state your recommendations for dealing with both the alleged victim and harasser.

Remember that your only real obligation as an investigator is to conduct an investigation impartially, fairly, and in good faith and to report your findings and conclusions accurately. Don't worry about being "right" or "wrong" when coming to a conclusion. The outcome of the investigation is secondary. The fact that you conducted a proper investigation based on the guidelines in this chapter is what counts.

Complete the Investigation With Follow-Up Action

When your report is completed, review it with the appropriate decision makers at your company and decide how, and by whom, your recommendations will be implemented. Time is still of the essence. Any corrective action against the alleged harasser must be taken promptly, and the alleged victim should be notified of that action. If you concluded that no sexual harassment occurred, you must meet separately with both the alleged victim and the accused to inform them of that decision and the reasons for your conclusion. Do not be second-guessed by either individual. Tell them that the decision is final, unless new evidence is presented.

Appropriate follow-up and corrective actions are discussed in detail in Chapter 6. For now, remember that the investigation will serve as the cornerstone for any action taken against the accused or accommodations for the victim.

Answers to "Test Your Knowledge"

1. *Lawyers are the best people to handle sexual harassment complaints because they know the law and how to interview witnesses.*

FALSE. Although lawyers may be an appropriate choice to handle some sexual harassment investigations (e.g., complex cases), they are not always the best choice depending on the company's organizational structure and budget. Management staff and outside consultants are also good choices. The individual needs to be impartial, have a working knowledge of sexual harassment law, be familiar with the company's policies, and have some training on proper interviewing techniques. Most in-house human resources professionals can easily meet these requirements.

2. *An employee who alleges sexual harassment against his or her direct supervisor should be transferred to another department while the investigation is being conducted.*

FALSE. Unless the employee asks for some type of accommodation, no such action should be taken. Changing a work schedule, transferring to another department, or requiring a leave of absence could be indications of retaliation and must be avoided without a request.

3. *An employer is under no legal obligation to continue a sexual harassment investigation if the complaining employee refuses to cooperate.*

FALSE. An employer must promptly investigate all sexual harassment complaints regardless of whether the complaining employee refuses to cooperate. The investigator should continue with the investigation and inform the complaining employee of that fact.

4. *An investigator should never review the personnel file of an accused harasser before an investigation begins because the information found could make the investigator biased.*

FALSE. Personnel records of the complaining employee and the accused should be reviewed by the investigator before an investigation begins to assess any reporting relationship between the parties (e.g., supervisor-subordinate), to determine whether there could be any ulterior motive for the complaint, and to learn any facts about the parties' past behaviors that might be relevant to the sexual harassment complaint. Although there is always a potential for bias, it is outweighed by the need for an investigator to prepare for the investigation armed with all available information.

5. *An investigator should tell a complaining employee during the initial interview whether his or her sexual harassment claim has any validity.*

FALSE. An investigator should never give an opinion or editorialize during an interview with the complaining employee or any witness. The investigation must be objective, based on specific facts, and not tainted by the investigator's initial subjective reactions.

6. *Rumors and office gossip are sources of information that an investigator should consider.*

TRUE. Although rumors and office gossip are not the best sources by far, they may lead the investigator to other witnesses or evidence that is credible and relevant.

7. *An employee complaining about sexual harassment should be required to sign a statement verifying that the investigator's interview notes are accurate.*

TRUE. The investigator should review his or her notes of the interview with the complaining employee, ask if they are accurate, and request that they be signed and dated. In this way, the investigator can be confident that the record of the facts of the complaint is accurate.

8. *An investigator should allow the accused harasser to blow off steam about the allegations during an initial interview.*

FALSE. The accused should stick to the facts and his or her version of the events. The interview of the accused should never turn into an investigation or assessment of the complaining employee.

9. *A witness's body language is helpful in determining his or her credibility.*

TRUE. Body language is helpful, although it may not be determinative of a witness's credibility. It is merely one factor, along with inconsistent or implausible statements, with which an investigator can attempt to assess whether an individual is telling the truth.

10. *The primary goal of any sexual harassment investigation is to come to the "right" conclusion.*

FALSE. The primary goal is to conduct a prompt, reasonable, and fair investigation in good faith. As long as the conclusion reached is reasonable based on the facts, there is no "right" conclusion.

Case Scenarios and Practical Guidance for the Real World

Scenario A

You are part of the sexual harassment investigation team at your company. When you try to arrange an interview with the complaining employee, he tells you that he doesn't want to be involved and that he has nothing more to say.

Practical Guidance

Employees who complain of sexual harassment and then refuse to cooperate with the investigation often fear retaliation by the alleged harasser, peers, or others. You should ask the employee why he does not want to cooperate and explain that there will be no reprisals or retaliation for doing so. Also stress that the alleged sexual harassment could reoccur without prompt action. More important, tell the employee that his refusal to cooperate may affect the outcome of the investigation and will be considered when deciding if sexual harassment really did take place. Finally, remember that you must still conduct a thorough investigation regardless of the complaining employee's cooperation or input. Interview other witnesses, including the accused, and meet again with the accuser after the investigation is concluded and a final outcome is reached.

Scenario B

You have followed all the steps for conducting a proper investigation but in the end, it boils down to a he said/she said situation and you are still not sure what really happened.

Practical Guidance

Conducting an investigation with a he said/she said conclusion is not unusual. Reexamine the facts, and carefully reconsider the evidence you have collected. If you need to conduct further interviews, do so to determine if you missed anything or if witness statements have changed in any way. You should try to avoid an inconclusive investigation result unless there is absolutely no way to make reasonable credibility determinations. If you are having trouble obtaining certain information or cooperation from witnesses, consider bringing in a third party to assist you, such as a lawyer or a consultant. Remember that your diligence in conducting the investigation is your most important job. Your methodology, professionalism, expediency, and good-faith effort will determine whether the organization responded appropriately.

Notes

1. See, e.g., *Brooms v. Regal Tube Co.*, 881 F.2d 412 (7th Cir. 1989).
2. See, e.g., *NLRB v. Weingarten, Inc.*, 420 U.S. 251 (1975).

CHAPTER 6

"A Slap on the Wrist or a Kick in the Pants?"
Taking Prompt and Effective Corrective Action

Taking in a sexual harassment complaint, gathering facts, interviewing witnesses, assessing credibility and motives, and documenting all the findings in a neatly packaged investigation report is only half the battle in the war against sexual harassment. To "win" the war, a company is legally obligated to take prompt and effective corrective action that will adequately punish the harasser, accommodate the victim, and prevent sexual harassment from occurring again.

Managers involved in the corrective action process should never take their responsibilities lightly. This is serious business, particularly when the U.S. Supreme Court has advanced such a restrictive view of the defenses available to employers in sexual harassment cases. Remember that in quid pro quo sexual harassment cases (e.g., tangible employment actions for a manager's sexual advances), there is no defense! An employer is absolutely liable. Even if a company takes corrective action after the fact, or claims ignorance about a manager's sexually harassing conduct, the company is on the hook. However, regardless of the liability issue, a company must still take appropriate corrective action to prevent and eradicate the effects of sexual harassment in the workplace.

On the other hand, a company has some chance to completely eliminate or reduce liability in hostile environment sexual harassment cases (e.g., severe and pervasive sexually offensive conduct with no tangible employment action) by taking prompt and effective corrective action. In these cases, the company has to prove two things: (1) that it exercised reasonable care to prevent and correct promptly any sexually harassing behavior and (2) that the complaining employee unreasonably failed to take advantage of any preventive or corrective opportunities provided by the employer's policy against sexual harassment or to otherwise avoid harm. Although both parts of the defense must be established in order to walk away from a sexual harassment case "home free," there is no way to prevail or reduce damages if the corrective action process is not done properly.

All managers need to know what type of corrective action is appropriate when a sexual harassment investigation is inconclusive, when no sexual harassment is found, when there is a false report of sexual harassment, and most important, when an investigation concludes that sexual harassment occurred. Even if you are not involved in the complaint or investigation process, one of the employees you supervise may be the victim or perpetrator of sexual harassment, and you may be asked to become involved in disciplinary decisions or other corrective actions necessary to conclude the matter. Therefore, it is essential for you to have a basic understanding of how and why certain disciplinary and corrective measures are imposed in sexual harassment cases.

Test Your Knowledge

Corrective action is the last important step in combating sexual harassment. Some of your managerial experiences of supervising and disciplining employees may come in handy, but sexual harassment is not a run-of-the mill offense. Do you know when to give "a slap on the wrist" or "a kick in the pants" for sexual harassment? Test your knowledge with the following true-or-false statements, putting a T (for true) or an F (for false) in front of each statement. Read the remainder of this chapter, answer the questions again, and compare your initial answers with those given at the end of the chapter.

True or False?

_____ 1. When a sexual harassment investigation results in an inconclusive outcome, it is necessary only to inform the parties in writing. No further corrective action is required in most cases.

_____ 2. A complaining employee suspected of filing a false report of sexual harassment should be immediately disciplined.

_____ 3. Always ask the victim of sexual harassment what he or she believes would be a proper remedy if sexual harassment is found.

_____ 4. An oral warning is usually the appropriate corrective action for an individual being disciplined for sexual harassment for the first time.

_____ 5. When deciding on the proper discipline for a perpetrator of sexual harassment, the individual's past disciplinary record is not really relevant unless there are infractions for past acts of sexual harassment.

_____ 6. A victim of sexual harassment should always be told how the harasser is being disciplined and what was stated to the harasser in a disciplinary meeting.

_____ 7. When sexual harassment is found and the victim and harasser work in the same department, a manager should make every attempt to transfer one of the individuals in order to minimize their contact.

_____ 8. Management should never disclose the facts of a sexual harassment investigation or the corrective action taken to anyone other than the victim, the harasser, and those managers who need to be directly involved.

_____ 9. A manager should always offer counseling options to a victim of sexual harassment whether or not it is requested.

_____ 10. Management must monitor the behavior of both the victim and the harasser after sexual harassment has been found and the harasser has been disciplined.

The Inconclusive Sexual Harassment Investigation

There will always be some cases when managers responsible for investigating sexual harassment cases are unable to make a determination from the evidence collected whether sexual harassment has occurred. Even when the investigation process goes smoothly, there may be credible witness statements on both sides, and the documentary evidence could point in a thousand different directions. Most managers at this point may be tempted to close the file and move on to other important matters. Unfortunately, the manager involved with sexual harassment investigations and the corrective action process still has some important responsibilities even in the face of an inconclusive investigation report.

Keep in mind that the whole point of a comprehensive sexual harassment prevention policy is to eradicate sexual harassment in the workplace. To achieve this goal and convince employees that the company is serious about preventing and correcting sexual harassment, appropriate follow-up action must be implemented after an investigation of any sexual harassment complaint, whether or not the allegations prove to be true or they simply amount to a mixed bag where no likely conclusions can be drawn. Both the complaining employee and the alleged harasser must be told about an inconclusive final investigation report in separate meetings with management. If you are the manager responsible for such a task, make sure you document any meetings or company actions with thorough note-taking and consider all of the following important factors.

Maintain Strict Neutrality

The biggest mistake a manager can make when meeting with either party to discuss an inconclusive sexual harassment investigation report is to give an impression that one individual's side of the story was somewhat more believable, notwithstanding the final outcome. Even if this is your gut reaction, keep it to yourself. Both parties must believe that you are being a neutral communicator, with no hidden agenda or suspicions. Tell the parties that the investigation was thorough, but that based on all the evidence, it is impossible to say whether sexual harassment did or did not occur.

Answer questions as accurately as you can, but never engage in arguments about the facts of the case or allow yourself to be second-guessed about the final outcome of the investigation. Tell the individuals that the outcome is final unless new evidence is presented. Leave the door open in this regard, but explain that the company will not rehash allegations and facts that have already been carefully reviewed. Never make excuses for the inconclusive outcome of the report or suggest that the investigation process was problematic or flawed in any way. When you maintain strict neutrality when discussing the outcome of the investigation, the complaining employee and the alleged harasser may not be happy with the result, but they will at least feel that the company did its best to conduct an impartial investigation and remedy the situation.

Reaffirm Zero Tolerance

After explaining the inconclusive results, review and reaffirm the company's sexual harassment prevention policy, with particular emphasis on the zero tolerance statement. Both parties should be told that despite the outcome of this case, the company is strongly committed to preventing and correcting all complaints of sexual harassment and to eliminating any inappropriate sexual behavior even if it does not rise to the level of sexual harassment in the legal sense.

Give both parties another copy of the policy, highlight the important points, and tell them to reread it. Discuss what zero tolerance really means: absolutely no inappropriate sexual behavior will ever be tolerated. Finally, explain that the sexual harassment complaint at issue was viewed as a serious matter and that all future complaints will be taken seriously by the company, with prompt and effective remedial action.

Stress "No Retaliation"

Both the complaining employee and the accused must be told once again that there will never be any reprisals or retaliation for complaining about sexual harassment. Tell the complaining employee to report immediately any activity that he or she may perceive to be retaliation and that management will investigate the report immediately and take whatever action is necessary. Similarly, explain to the accused that there will be no reprisals by the company based on the fact that a sexual harassment complaint was made. However, the accused, particularly if he or she is a manager, must be warned that any acts of retaliation against the complaining employee will be met with discipline, up to and including termination.

Naturally, someone accused of sexual harassment will be upset and somewhat defensive, regardless of the ultimate outcome of an investigation. When the investigation is inconclusive, the accused may be even more defensive because the outcome did not achieve a complete acquittal of the charges, and he or she may believe that a dark cloud will hang overhead in the minds of coworkers. You need to be sensitive to this problem, while at the same time giving a stern warning that any attempts to get even or lash out at the complaining employee in any manner will not be tolerated and will be met with discipline.

Encourage Complaints

Employees who are told that the outcome of their sexual harassment complaint and the investigation process is inconclusive will undoubtedly be disappointed and still believe that their allegations are valid. They also may worry that any future sexual harassment complaints will be dismissed by the company or that complaining about inappropriate sexual conduct is futile. As a manager confronting this problem, you must inform the employee that because there was conflicting evidence and thus no firm conclusion about the sexual harassment at issue, the company is not discounting the claims or questioning the complaining employee's belief that the alleged events did in fact occur.

You must make the point that the company encourages employees to come forward with all complaints of sexual harassment and that every case will be carefully considered on its own facts. Tell the complaining employee not to be discouraged about the outcome of the case and to report any future observations of inappropriate sexual conduct promptly. And explain to the accused that the sexual harassment complaint procedure is still in full swing and that any new reports about his or her conduct will be taken seriously, investigated, and punished if true.

Explore Accommodation Issues

An inconclusive sexual harassment investigation often creates an impression that the issues are left dangling, with no company action. To combat this problem, both the complaining employee and the accused should be asked whether they have any opinion or suggestion on how to proceed. The complaining employee or the accused may request a job transfer to another department or a revised work schedule so that both parties will have less contact. Additionally, one of the parties may suggest that sensitivity and sexual harassment training should be required to alleviate tensions, improve awareness, and prevent the occurrence of future conduct that could be construed as sexually offensive.

Depending on the circumstances, the company should consider all suggestions for accommodating both the complaining employee and the accused. Although the investigation was inconclusive, there still may be animosities between the parties and potential for disruption in the workplace because of it. However, never lose sight of the fact that it is the company that will ultimately decide whether to make any accommodations and which accommodations are appropriate. The parties should be informed of this fact while being told that their suggestions are appreciated and that the company will make every effort to implement an accommodation when necessary.

Monitor the Workforce

Tell the parties that the company will continue to monitor the workforce for signs of sexual harassment and that an inconclusive investigation does not mean that management will fall asleep on the job in this regard. Make sure you explain that neither will not be singled out in any manner, but that management will be on high alert now that a complaint was lodged, despite the inconclusive outcome.

After you have this discussion with both parties, make sure you follow through. Again, it is important to stress and act on the company's commitment to preventing sexual harassment, encouraging complaints, thoroughly investigating all claims, and taking appropriate corrective action to stop sexual harassment from ever occurring in the workplace.

Final Words of Caution

Dealing with sexual harassment complaints and the investigation process is never easy. There will always be cases of he said/she said or other conflicting statements and evidence that are difficult to decipher and even more difficult to reconcile. In going through the process, you must never lose sight of the fact that no sexual harassment case will ever be clear-cut. There will always be hard decisions to make involving people with whom you may have to work every day.

Because of the nature of the subject, it is much easier to go through the motions and announce that an investigation is inconclusive in order to avoid the decisions that need to be made in furtherance of the company's sexual harassment prevention policy.

Never make this mistake. The inconclusive investigation should always be the exception, never the rule. A series of inconclusive investigations will be perceived by employees as management's way of perhaps meeting its legal obligations but dodging the choices that would ultimately ensure a workplace free of sexual harassment.

No Finding of Sexual Harassment

When an investigation results in a finding that no sexual harassment has occurred, the managers involved must ask themselves one very important question: "Was this a legitimate sexual harassment complaint or a deliberate false report?" The answer to this question will determine how a manager should react and the actions that the company needs to take.

The Legitimate Complaint

The legitimate sexual harassment complaint involves an honest difference in interpretation about the events that gave rise to the claim. For example, suppose a female employee works in a small research facility where the equipment is set up in such a way that employees must stand only a few inches apart when testing products. She alleges that one of her male coworkers consistently brushes up against her in a sexually offensive manner. After investigating the claim, the evidence shows that the male employee was not even aware that he had brushed up against the employee and the company ultimately decides that the physical contact was inadvertent because of the laboratory equipment and the need for employees to work in close proximity.

Obviously this is a situation where there was an honest difference in interpretation by the complaining employee and the accused. The complaining employee truly believed that the physical contact was sexually offensive, and the accused was unaware that he was even engaging in the conduct alleged.

In legitimate complaint cases, you need to meet separately with the complaining employee and the accused in much the same way as was done with meetings to discuss the inconclusive investigation. Again, take good notes and document everything said for the investigation file. Begin by advising the parties that the decision was made based solely on the evidence presented. You must then clearly explain the reasons that the company found no sexual harassment, stressing the important details of the investigation report.

In this regard, be as specific as possible. For example, if the witnesses' statements did not support the complaining employee's version of events, let both parties know. If the investigation team believed, based on all the evidence, that the complaining employee's statements were inconsistent, make that fact known and point out the inconsistencies. If there were serious doubt and no credible evidence that the conduct complained about was unwelcome, the parties should be told. The point is to buttress your decision by highlighting the important evidence so that the parties will know that the company's decision was based on a reasonable and good-faith interpretation of all the facts.

In addition, remain neutral by simply discussing the evidence and the result without commentary or personal opinions. Never allow yourself to become argumentative or to be second-guessed about the outcome. Stress that the decision is final unless new evidence is submitted. Moreover, you must go over the company's sexual harassment prevention policy, highlighting the zero tolerance statement, encouraging sexual harassment complaints, assuring the parties of no retaliation, and reviewing the complaint, investigation, and corrective action process.

The False Report

A false report usually involves evidence that the complaining employee has some ulterior motive for making a sexual harassment claim backed up by other credible evidence that the complaint was false. For example, a male employee alleges that his supervisor keeps making sexual advances and lewd comments about his sex life. The investigation uncovers that the employee had recently received a three-day suspension for performance problems and that he had had a loud argument with the supervisor about it on the day before he filed his sexual harassment complaint. Witness statements directly contradict all the facts alleged by the complaining employee, and he even changes his story after being confronted with what the witnesses said. After considering all the evidence, the company makes a determination that the complaining employee deliberately made a dishonest and false report of sexual harassment.

In these cases, disciplinary action should be taken against the complaining employee to discourage him or her from making future false reports and to send a message that false reports of sexual harassment will not be tolerated. However, you must proceed with extreme caution when dealing with discipline for a false report to avoid claims of retaliation by the complaining employee. Make sure your evidence is airtight and that you have documented all the facts that support your conclusion that the employee's allegations were deliberately dishonest. If the evidence is clear, meaning you think you can prove it, the employee should be disciplined in accordance with any company policy dealing with dishonesty or with the same level of discipline given to other employees who have previously engaged in similar misconduct.

Finally, never discipline an employee for filing a charge of discrimination with the EEOC or a companion state agency that handles employment discrimination cases. Doing so is a clear violation of the antiretaliation provisions of Title VII or state laws, and the company will be found liable for imposing discipline unlawfully. If a charge is pending when you conclude that a sexual harassment complaint was a deliberate false report, contact the agency investigating the sexual harassment charge and immediately submit your evidence in writing.

Sexual Harassment Found

When the evidence supports a finding of sexual harassment, the company has a legal obligation to take prompt and appropriate disciplinary action that furthers the goal of eradicating sexual harassment in the workplace. Merely telling someone "Never do it again" is not enough to achieve that goal or to convince a court that corrective action was in fact meaningful or adequate. Deciding on the proper corrective action and implementing it in the right way takes more than a knee-jerk response. There is no substitute for careful thought and planning.

It is also important to remember that the company is the ultimate decision maker. Although discussions with a victim or harasser may lead to options regarding some aspects of the corrective action process, they should never be relied on as a substitute for the company's judgment. Similarly, you should understand that the company's ultimate decision in a case where sexual harassment is found will never please everyone. The victim will usually think that the harasser deserves stronger punishment, and the harasser will almost always believe that he or she is being punished too harshly. Other employees who get wind of the situation may volunteer their opinions, and managers may not always agree on the type of discipline or other remedial action to impose.

Nevertheless, the company and the managers involved in the corrective action process must decide on (1) appropriate punishment for the harasser, (2) adequate accommodation for the victim, and (3) proper follow-up actions to deter sexual harassment in the future and prevent retaliation. If these three tasks are taken seriously and done right, even the naysayers will have to recognize that the company acted fairly, reasonably, and in good faith when making its decisions about corrective action.

Discipline for the Harasser

The guiding principle for deciding how to discipline a sexual harasser is to ensure that the punishment fits the crime. In quid pro quo sexual harassment cases, this decision is usually clear. Any manager who makes a sexual advance to a subordinate, followed by a termination or some other tangible job penalty when those advances are rejected, deserves to be fired, and fired fast, in most cases. The more difficult decisions come about when considering the appropriate discipline for an individual who has engaged in hostile-environment sexual harassment.

Someone who makes a few off-color sexual jokes should not receive the same penalty as someone who repeatedly grabs the buttocks of a coworker. Making sure that the punishment fits the crime in these cases requires a careful review of the facts, an analysis of the disciplinary options available, and consideration of how other disciplinary matters were handled in the past by the company. Fairness, consistency, and common sense should all come into play.

A Smorgasbord of Discipline

As a manager, you have probably had your fair share of disciplinary problems with the employees you supervise. You may already know that many companies implement what is commonly referred to as progressive discipline when deciding how to deal with an employee who can't follow the rules. Progressive discipline involves giving more severe penalties as the employee continues to have disciplinary problems. The rationale is that the employee can eventually be rehabilitated and may refrain from repeating the same or other improper conduct when a threat of greater punishment is looming overhead.

Typically an employee subjected to progressive discipline receives an oral warning for a first offense. If a second offense is committed, a more formal, written warning is issued. As the employee continues to violate company rules, a suspension may be imposed, and ultimately the discharge penalty. When certain serious disciplinary problems arise, such as theft or violence, termination is probably the only alternative.

As a general proposition, progressive discipline should not be ignored in sexual harassment cases. The sexual harasser who told off-color sexual jokes should probably not be fired if it was a first offense and he or she had an otherwise exemplary employment record. Some other form of discipline should be implemented, although a simple verbal warning would probably not be sufficient. If the same conduct occurs again, you must reassess the situation and decide whether a more severe penalty short of termination is appropriate, or if termination is the only recourse. In contrast, the sexual harasser who engages in unwelcome physical contact or a physical assault should probably be fired in most cases. Here the conduct is egregious.

Although the principles of progressive discipline should be considered when deciding how to punish the sexual harasser, the type of discipline to impose cannot always be chosen from the standard progressive discipline menu. Rarely will the sexual harassment dilemma be solved by limiting yourself to the four most common types of progressive discipline: an oral warning, a written warning, a suspension, and discharge. Although these types of discipline are appropriate in some sexual harassment cases, there is usually a need for more varied choices to effectuate meaningful and adequate corrective action.

For example, one or more of the following types of discipline may be appropriate to punish a sexual harasser, depending on the circumstances:

- Demotion
- Denial of prospective promotion

- Denial of prospective pay increase

- Job transfer

- Shift reassignment

- Pay reduction

- Instructions not to be alone with or talk to the victim

- Mandatory sensitivity training or counseling

- A formal apology to the victim

There are many other forms of discipline, including combinations of those listed above, which will need to be tailored to the facts of a case.

Two additional points about discipline and corrective action for the sexual harasser should be considered. First, oral warnings are usually inappropriate and unreliable in these cases. They are not taken very seriously by employees, and if you ultimately have to appear in court or before the EEOC, there will be no record to prove that you took appropriate corrective action. Thus, if an oral warning is required for some reason, prepare a signed written memorandum for the sexual harassment investigation file stating when and where you gave the oral warning and the content of that warning.

Second, don't forget that a comprehensive sexual harassment prevention policy should prohibit all inappropriate sexual conduct, regardless of whether the conduct is sexual harassment in the legal sense. The receptionist who tells a dirty joke in front of customers in the waiting room or the sales manager who calls one of his subordinates a "bitch" when angry have both engaged in inappropriate conduct that should not be tolerated and for which discipline should be imposed. Thus, all managers should be prepared to consider some form of discipline for these infractions to promote the company's zero tolerance policy.

Factors for Deciding the Level of Discipline

There are several important factors to consider when making a decision on how tough you will be. Review and assess the following factors every time you make a disciplinary decision involving a sexual harasser, while keeping in mind that the punishment must be appropriate.

- *Severity of conduct.* How egregious or severe was the sexual harassment? Did it involve physical contact or a physical assault? What type of harm did the victim suffer? Was it physical harm? Emotional? Loss of a promotion or key assignment? All these questions need to be answered when trying to determine the severity of the conduct and deciding on the proper discipline. The more severe the conduct was, the more severe the penalty should be.

- *Frequency of conduct.* Was the sexual harassment pervasive or rare? Was it repeated and continuous, or one sexually offensive incident when an individual used bad judgment? The employee who makes derogatory sexual remarks about women every day for three months will require far greater punishment than the employee who made two or three similar remarks over a two-week period. The greater the frequency of the improper conduct was, the greater the penalty should be.

- *Notice of policy.* Did the sexual harasser have prior notice of the company's sexual harassment prevention policy? Hopefully, the answer to this question will be yes. When the company has done the proper work, all employees will have received the policy and signed an acknowledgment form that they read and understood it. Thus, the harasser can never argue that he or she was unaware of the policy or that a violation of the policy could result in discipline. If the answer to this question is no, the company will face some serious problems when deciding how to discipline the individual or if confronted with a lawsuit by the accused.

- *Prior employment record.* No disciplinary action should ever be taken against a sexual harasser, or any other employee for that matter, without first reviewing the employee's overall employment record and past disciplinary infractions. Unless the sexual harassment at issue involved a physical assault or other egregious physical contact, something short of termination will most likely be the resulting discipline. Generally, if the harasser is an exemplary employee with no prior history of violating company rules, common sense dictates that the punishment will not be as severe as it would be for a chronic or prior rule violator.

- *Company's past practice.* Has the company experienced other similar incidents of sexual harassment where a sexual harasser was disciplined? If so, the same type of discipline should be imposed for the harasser at issue. A company must be consistent when deciding on appropriate corrective action. If one sexual harasser is given a two-day suspension for repeatedly making lewd sexual comments, while another is terminated for the same conduct without some good reason, the company is setting itself up for a possible discrimination or wrongful discharge lawsuit. Past practice and a comparison of the levels of discipline given for other offenders must be considered before making a final decision on discipline in a given case.

  Moreover, you need to be consistent with discipline from the standpoint of the harasser's gender, race, age, or other "protected class." For example, terminating a female employee for grabbing a male coworker's buttocks, but not terminating a male employee who grabs a coworker's breast, could lead to a sex discrimination case. Assuming all other factors are equal (e.g., disciplinary history, notice of policy), similar offensive conduct must result in similar discipline, regardless of the individual's other characteristics.

- *Prior remedial steps.* Has the harasser been disciplined for violating any company rules in the past, and did the discipline imposed have any effect? Someone who has been receptive to prior discipline by improving his or her conduct may deserve less severe punishment for sexual harassment because he or she is a candidate for rehabilitation. In contrast, when prior remedial steps have had no effect on an employee's behavior, including past violations of the company's sexual harassment policy, it is probably doubtful that a more mild form of punishment (e.g., sensitivity training) will have any effect. Thus, if prior discipline was unsuccessful, you probably should impose harsher sanctions in an attempt to ensure effectiveness.

- *Potential for behavioral changes.* Has the harasser displayed any level of contrition, remorse, or openness to changing sexually offensive behaviors? If you are dealing with a harasser who remains angry, defensive, and unapologetic even in the face of solid evidence, there is little potential for change. On the other hand, someone who realizes the wrongs committed and sincerely wants to "make it right" should be given more deference when it comes to deciding on the appropriate punishment. You should always consider a bona fide and effective educational program for the harasser as part of a corrective action plan. This means using trained professionals to counsel and educate the harasser on sexual harassment issues and personal behavior, rather than relying on in-house personnel to do the job.

Simply telling an individual "Times have changed," "Avoid the person," or "We don't want any more problems" is no substitute for formal training on unacceptable conduct. Requiring mandatory attendance at educational programs can always be coupled with other forms of discipline when the harasser is not being terminated. There will never be any change in conduct if the harasser "just doesn't get it."

- *Compliance with other company policies.* Never ignore other company policies concerning discipline that may be independent from the company's sexual harassment prevention policy. If certain general grievance steps or progressive discipline procedures have been adopted, you must follow them or attempt to reconcile them with the disciplinary statements in the sexual harassment prevention policy. For example, if a general rules violation policy states that an employee will not be disciplined before attending a meeting with the human resources director or other management official, make sure you follow that policy before imposing any discipline for sexual harassment. Similarly, be aware of any union contracts or an employment agreement with the harasser that could somehow affect or limit your disciplinary decisions.

- *Management levels.* Should the company require different standards of conduct and impose different types of discipline for sexual harassment by managers who occupy higher positions of authority within the company? In other words, should a vice president who commits sexual harassment be treated differently and be held to a higher standard of conduct than a first-line supervisor who commits the same act? Interestingly, the U.S. Supreme Court in *Burlington Industries, Inc. v. Ellerth* made note of the fact that the supervisor who sexually harassed Kimberly Ellerth in that case was only a "mid-level manager."[1]

Because there was no tangible employment action taken against *Ellerth,* the Court treated the manager's sexual advances and other sexually offensive conduct as hostile-environment sexual harassment. Thus, the employer was permitted to raise a defense, and liability was not absolute. However, the Court left open the question of whether liability for severe and pervasive sexual conduct by top-level or high-ranking managers could be absolute even without a tangible employment action.

If a company is truly serious about zero tolerance and setting a strong example for the complete elimination of sexual harassment in the workplace, then perhaps holding upper management to a higher standard makes sense. However, this is an issue that should be carefully reviewed before you are at the point of making a final decision on proper corrective action for sexual harassment in a particular case so that all managers and employees will have prior notice of the possible ramifications.

Disciplinary Interview With the Harasser

Once the final disciplinary decision is made, you must have a face-to-face interview with the harasser to inform him or her of the decision. It is preferable to have another management representative present to be a witness and to take detailed notes, with copies subsequently placed in both the investigation file and the harasser's personnel file. Everything said at the meeting should be written down. Never communicate your disciplinary decision in a written memorandum or letter to the harasser without a meeting, even if the discipline being imposed is a discharge. Despite the nature of the conduct or your personal opinions about the sexual harassment incident, the harasser must still be treated with professionalism.

The harasser may insist on having a lawyer present at a disciplinary interview. From the company's perspective, it is usually not preferable to have lawyers present at any employee interview in order to avoid creating an adversarial or confrontational atmosphere. However, you should grant an individual's request for legal counsel in a disciplinary interview for sexual harassment because of the serious nature of the offense or if you are obligated to do so by law. And if you do grant the harasser's request, make sure you arrange for the company's legal counsel to be present as well. For additional information on the issue of legal representation, review the "Interviewing the Accused" section in Chapter 5.

Always begin the disciplinary interview by reviewing the allegations made in the sexual harassment complaint. Then explain how the investigation was conducted and the results of the investigation. Don't make statements such as, "You have been found guilty" or, "We've concluded that you are a sexual harasser." Simply tell the individual that based solely on all the evidence presented, it is the company's position that sexual harassment has occurred and that discipline is necessary to prevent sexual harassment from occurring in the future. Do express strong disapproval for the harasser's conduct and remind him or her that it clearly violated the company's sexual harassment prevention policy.

If the harasser has questions about the evidence or the company's conclusions, answer them as accurately as possible. Never argue about the evidence or the company's decision. The purpose of the disciplinary interview is not to rehash the facts or consider last minute pleas from the harasser. Make it clear that the decision is final based on the evidence and that the outcome of the investigation or the disciplinary action being implemented will not be second-guessed.

Then fully explain the discipline being imposed and why that discipline was chosen. For example, if sensitivity training or counseling is being required, tell the individual that education and awareness of the problem are necessary in order to work on changing inappropriate behaviors. Similarly, if a three-day suspension is being given because the harasser's conduct did not improve after a one-day suspension for similar conduct in the past, explain the rationale behind the decision. Make it clear that harsher discipline, including a possible discharge, will be imposed if the conduct ever occurs again. Also, firmly state that retaliation against the victim will not be tolerated and will most likely result in discharge.

In all cases you must provide the harasser with another copy of the company's sexual harassment prevention policy and review each provision line by line. Stress the company's zero tolerance statement and the definition and examples of inappropriate sexual conduct. Highlight the disciplinary provisions, again stating the potential consequences of further violations. Discuss the company's legal obligations to prevent and correct the problem and the duties and responsibilities of all employees to report sexual harassment whenever they observe it.

Your discussion of the sexual harassment prevention policy must also include statements about the confidentiality provisions. Assure the harasser that confidentiality has been maintained by the company to the greatest extent possible. Explain that the company will continue to keep the matter confidential and that the harasser must do the same. In this regard, the company should rarely go public with the details of the sexual harassment investigation or the discipline being imposed to protect against a possible defamation lawsuit by the harasser. Only in certain limited circumstances, such as those discussed in "Whom to Tell?" later in this chapter, should such information be more widely disclosed.

Finally, end the disciplinary interview in an upbeat fashion. Words of encouragement will go a lot further at this point than more words of admonishment. Tell the harasser that the company has faith in his or her ability to change and to correct inappropriate behaviors. Be sincere, and offer management's assistance in this regard whenever possible.

Closure Interview and Remedial Action for the Victim

After meeting with the harasser, you must immediately conduct a closure interview with the victim to discuss the outcome of the investigation and the company's corrective actions. Again, this meeting should be documented, with detailed written notes placed in the investigation file. The victim should be told that the harasser was disciplined and that he or she was strongly warned about future inappropriate conduct. Explain that the company believes its disciplinary decision will prevent future incidents and that the victim must inform the company immediately of any reoccurrence of sexual harassment by anyone. If the victim disagrees in any way, he or she should be permitted to voice an opinion and follow up with a written objection for the file.

The victim also must be advised of the company's position on confidentiality. It should be stressed that the company has maintained confidentiality to the greatest extent possible concerning all aspects of the complaint, investigation, and final outcome. The victim should be told that all parties involved must continue to maintain confidentiality and not disclose any information about the matter to anyone without a need to know.

Taking appropriate corrective action also involves taking meaningful remedial action on behalf of the victim. Basically the victim needs to be "made whole" for any losses suffered as a result of the sexual harassment. This could entail correcting erroneous personnel documents (e.g., performance reviews), reinstating lost wages or benefits arising out of stress-related absences due to the harassment, reinstating a lost job opportunity or promotion, reimbursement for psychiatric counseling or other medical bills, and correcting a host of other potential harms. These matters must be explored and resolved during the closure interview with the victim.

The victim may require some other job accommodation to cope with the effects of the sexual harassment. Job transfers, reassignments, shift or schedule changes, and other workplace restructuring efforts may need to be implemented. However, to avoid retaliation claims, never take action in this regard without first consulting with the victim. Ask the victim directly what, if anything, would be helpful to make the work environment more comfortable.

Many managers make the mistake of ordering a job accommodation based on their first instinctive reaction: to place the victim and the harasser as far apart as possible. This may not be an appropriate job accommodation and could lead to a claim of retaliation by the victim. For example, there may be circumstances where the victim's job satisfaction far outweighs his or her need to avoid contact with the harasser. Thus, you need to cover all the options for a possible job accommodation with as much input as possible from the victim.

Moreover, the company should offer post-harassment counseling to the victim. Many victims of sexual harassment do not request such counseling because they are embarrassed or they want to give the impression that they can "handle it." Consequently, you should strongly encourage prearranged counseling options and advise the victim that the company will pay for this service. This will not only assist the victim in alleviating the effects of sexual harassment, it will play well with all employees and add credibility to the company's sexual harassment prevention policy.

Appropriate Follow-Up Actions

It is extremely important to follow up consistently with both the harasser and the victim after the complaint has been resolved. This is particularly true if the victim and harasser have remained in the same department or in close physical proximity in the workplace. You need to make sure that the discipline has been effective, the situation has been completely remedied, and the victim has not been subjected to any retaliation. The best way to accomplish this task is by scheduling periodic meetings with both parties to monitor and discuss their behaviors. This should be done at least once per month over the next six months unless the circumstances warrant more or less time. And never forget to make a record of all follow-up actions.

At meetings with the victim, ask whether the harassment has ceased or if there has been any retaliation by the harasser; take action immediately if there are any problems. Follow up with questions about any job accommodations that may have been implemented and the status of counseling. Make sure the victim feels that you are being sincere and that the company is still taking the sexual harassment issue seriously. Answer all questions from the victim, and continue to offer the company's assistance in dealing with sexual harassment issues.

When meeting with the harasser, reinforce good behavior by offering positive comments if there have been no complaints. Obtain an update on the harasser's efforts to change his or her behavior through sexual harassment sensitivity or training sessions. Ask the harasser if additional counseling would be helpful, and discuss the reasons for the answer given. Encourage a periodic review of the company's sexual harassment prevention policy and confirm that you will always be available to answer any questions about the issue.

Whom to Tell?

Confidentiality needs to be maintained to the greatest extent possible, with disclosure typically made only to those individuals with a need to know: the victim, the harasser, the manager taking the complaint, the manager(s) investigating the complaint, and other managers who may need to be consulted when making disciplinary decisions. Generally third-party witnesses need to know only the facts that involve them. Similarly, only managers with some direct involvement, not the whole management staff, need to be informed.

In some circumstances, certain witnesses, a department or work group, or even the entire workforce may need to be advised of the outcome of a sexual harassment investigation and the corrective action taken. For example, if hostile-environment sexual harassment involves several employees in a department, including the manager, other employees in the department may be adversely affected and lose faith in the company's sexual harassment prevention policy if they think nothing is being done about the problem.

Consequently, it may be necessary to advise an entire work group about certain sexual harassment allegations and the discipline eventually imposed to deter future sexual harassment and to create confidence in the employer's investigation and corrective action procedures. If a company's breach of confidentiality is ever challenged in these circumstances, a credible argument could be made that the entire work group had a need to know. However, management must be careful to weigh the benefits of making wider disclosures about sexual harassment complaints with the need to avoid defamation or other legal claims by the parties directly involved.

When the Harasser Fights Back

A company's worries about sexual harassment do not end even after the matter has been investigated, the harasser has been disciplined, the victim has been accommodated, and follow-up actions are proceeding smoothly. Some individuals accused of sexual harassment, however, will fight vigorously, especially when they have been disciplined or discharged for such an offense. The harasser who fights back usually perceives or has evidence that the company's sexual harassment investigation was done improperly or unfairly, the discipline imposed was unjust, the company was negligent, or it engaged in some other wrongful act such as disclosing information to third parties that adversely affected the perpetrator's reputation and future job prospects.

Perhaps the most famous case brought by an accused sexual harasser who decided to fight back is *MacKenzie v. Miller Brewer Company*.[2] Jerold MacKenzie had been employed as a manager for the

Miller Brewer Company in Milwaukee for many years. One morning he came into work and asked one of his female friends and coworkers whether she had seen an episode of the *Seinfeld* television show the night before. When she said that she had not, he proceeded to tell her about the story line. The episode centered around Jerry Seinfeld's inability to remember his date's name, recalling only that it rhymed with a part of the female anatomy. When MacKenzie told his female coworker the name, she claimed that she was offended and made a formal complaint of sexual harassment. After an investigation uncovered some other inappropriate sexual remarks by MacKenzie, he was fired by the company.

MacKenzie sued the company, the female employee who complained, and his direct supervisor, based on several legal theories, including wrongful termination, negligence, damage to reputation, and emotional distress. The gist of his claim was that the company mishandled the sexual harassment investigation and terminated him without cause. A jury ultimately awarded MacKenzie $27,103,000 in damages, of which over $20 million was earmarked as punitive damages, that is, damages assessed for pure punishment, against the employer.

Although the *MacKenzie* case is most often cited because of the immense monetary award, it clearly illustrates the perils employers face when attempting to follow the law on sexual harassment. However, if you use common sense, keep all facts close to the vest, and make sure the punishment fits the crime, you should be able to defend yourself or, better yet, deter lawsuits from ever being filed by the alleged victim or the accused.

Checklist for Corrective Action

Use the following checklist to jog your memory when deciding on appropriate discipline and implementing other corrective action decisions after a sexual harassment investigation is concluded.

Inconclusive Investigation

❏ Meet with the victim and harasser.

❏ Stay neutral, and explain the reason for the decision ("based on the evidence presented").

❏ State that the decision is final unless there is new evidence.

❏ Review the sexual harassment prevention policy in detail.

❏ Encourage complaints and stress no retaliation.

❏ Explore job accommodation issues with both parties.

❏ Follow up by monitoring the conduct of the accused.

No Sexual Harassment Found

❏ Determine if the complaint was legitimate or false.

❏ Consider discipline for the complainant victim if the complaint was false.

❏ Meet with the victim and the harasser.

❏ Stay neutral, and explain the reasons for the decision ("based on evidence").

❏ State that the decision was final.

❏ Review the sexual harassment prevention policy in detail.

❏ Encourage complaints, and stress no retaliation.

❏ Explore job accommodation issues with both parties.

❏ Follow up by monitoring the conduct of both parties.

Sexual Harassment Found

❏ Decide on harasser discipline:

- There must be no "knee-jerk" reactions.
- The punishment must fit the crime.
- Review prior employment records and the company's practice.
- Apply progressive discipline, if appropriate.
- Consider the potential for behavioral changes.

❏ Meet with the harasser:

- Have another manager present.
- Consider requests for legal representation.
- Review allegations and the rationale for discipline.
- Explain that the discipline is final.
- Warn against future misconduct and retaliation against the victim.
- Review the sexual harassment prevention policy in detail.
- Stress the confidentiality of the outcome.

- Offer encouragement for changing behavior.
❏ Meet with the victim:
    - Explain the decision and discipline given.
    - Stress confidentiality.
    - Consider "make-whole" remedies.
    - Explore job accommodations with the victim.
    - Suggest counseling to help the victim cope with the effects of the sexual harassment.
❏ Engage in follow-up actions:
    - Monitor all conduct.
    - Hold monthly meetings with the victim and the harasser.
    - Check for repeated sexual harassment.
    - Check for retaliation.
    - Check on job accommodations.
    - Reinforce good conduct.
    - Punish bad conduct.
❏ Always document everything with detailed notes for the investigation file.

Corrective Action Don'ts

When trying to take appropriate corrective action, sometimes a manager's instinctive reactions prompt the wrong decision and make matters worse. Corrective action takes careful thought and planning. Thus, when dealing with the issue, heed these don'ts:

- ✗ DON'T immediately fire someone who has engaged in sexual harassment.
- ✗ DON'T substitute good judgment and hard decisions with an inconclusive report.
- ✗ DON'T be second-guessed by either party about the final corrective action decisions.
- ✗ DON'T ignore the victim's needs when taking corrective action.

✗ DON'T automatically assume that a victim filed a false report when no harassment is found.

✗ DON'T fail to review an individual's prior employment record when deciding on discipline.

✗ DON'T force a victim to transfer jobs or change shifts to minimize contact with a harasser.

✗ DON'T ignore a harasser's potential for changing behaviors when considering discipline.

✗ DON'T state to a harasser things like, "You are a sexual harasser" or "You are guilty!"

✗ DON'T argue with either party about the facts or conclusion of an investigation.

✗ DON'T fail to review carefully the company's sexual harassment policy with both parties.

Answers to "Test Your Knowledge"

1. *When a sexual harassment investigation results in an inconclusive outcome, it is only necessary to inform the parties in writing. No further corrective action is required in most cases.*

FALSE. Always announce the outcome during a private face-to-face meeting with each party, and explain that based on the evidence, the company was unable to determine whether sexual harassment occurred. Corrective action in these circumstances involves reviewing the company's sexual harassment prevention policy with both parties and reaffirming the zero tolerance statement, prohibition against retaliation, and complaint procedure. It also involves exploring ways to increase awareness about inappropriate conduct.

2. *A complaining employee suspected of filing a false report of sexual harassment should be immediately disciplined.*

FALSE. Never discipline anyone based on a suspicion of wrongful conduct. Make sure that a suspected false report is not merely an honest difference in interpretation between two individuals who legitimately perceived events in different ways. Implement discipline only when your evidence of a false report is airtight.

3. *Always ask the victim of sexual harassment what he or she believes would be a proper remedy when sexual harassment is found.*

TRUE. However, you should never base your disciplinary decisions solely on the victim's suggestions or comments, and it should be made clear to all parties that the company is the ultimate decision maker and that their suggestions may not be appropriate or implemented.

4. *An oral warning is usually the appropriate corrective action for an individual being disciplined for sexual harassment for the first time.*

FALSE. Oral warnings are usually given for the most minor of offenses, and it would be difficult to imagine any case of sexual harassment where an oral warning would be appropriate even for the first offense. Moreover, oral warnings are unreliable as proof of corrective action unless they are converted to writing.

5. *When deciding on the proper discipline for a perpetrator of sexual harassment, the individual's past disciplinary record is not really relevant unless there are infractions for past acts of sexual harassment.*

FALSE. An individual's past disciplinary record is always relevant, no matter what the offense. Someone who repeatedly violates other rules and has a poor disciplinary record may require harsher discipline even for a first offense of sexual harassment than someone with an exemplary employment record.

6. *A victim of sexual harassment should always be told how the harasser is being disciplined and what was stated to the harasser in a disciplinary meeting.*

TRUE. The victim must be told precisely what the company is doing with regard to corrective action, which includes the discipline being imposed and any warnings or other statements about any future incidents of sexual harassment made to the harasser during a disciplinary meeting.

7. *When sexual harassment is found and the victim and harasser work in the same department, a manager should make every*

attempt to transfer one of the individuals in order to minimize their contact.

FALSE. Never take any action against either party without first exploring the possibility of a retaliation claim. In the case of the victim, the victim should be asked whether any job accommodations are necessary before any action is taken.

8. *Management should never disclose the facts of a sexual harassment investigation or the corrective action taken to anyone other than the victim, the harasser, and those managers who need to be directly involved.*

FALSE. In some circumstances it may be necessary to disclose such information to a department of employees or the entire workforce in cases where hostile-environment sexual harassment is rampant or affecting many employees, or when managers are involved in the conduct and the company needs to impress on the workforce that corrective action has been implemented.

9. *A manager should always offer counseling options to a victim of sexual harassment, whether or not it is requested.*

TRUE. Postharassment counseling at the company's expense should always be offered to help the victim alleviate the effects of sexual harassment.

10. *Management must monitor the behavior of both the victim and the harasser after sexual harassment has been found and the harasser has been disciplined.*

TRUE. Part of the obligation to take appropriate corrective action involves monitoring the parties to ensure that sexual harassment is not occurring again and that there has been no retaliation against the victim.

Case Scenarios and Practical Guidance for the Real World

Scenario A

A senior executive with a sterling performance record was accused of making gender-specific derogatory remarks about the female employees in the

company. Several women complained and cooperated in the investigation. The executive admitted making the remarks, apologized, and was generally remorseful about his behavior. However, he insisted that he meant no harm and that the complaining women overreacted.

Practical Guidance

Where an executive or any other employee has a good performance record and there are no prior acts of sexual harassment, discipline and other corrective actions need to be appropriate. Here, termination is not the proper choice, particularly since the executive apologized and was generally remorseful. However, making excuses for the inappropriate sexual comments needs to be addressed with the executive through sensitivity and sexual harassment training or individual counseling. A three- to four-week counseling program to raise awareness about general stereotypes and built-in biases would be one option. In any event, assist the executive with making the necessary behavioral changes and at the same time advise him that he could lose his job if he makes such comments again in the future.

Scenario B

A manager with a high potential for success in your organization is slated for a promotion to manage a key department. He recently returned from a business trip, where he landed a large new account. His manager praised his hard work and the results he achieved with the clients. However, a female manager who accompanied him on the trip had a different story to tell. She lodged a sexual harassment complaint, alleging that the manager made denigrating comments about women when the two of them were at dinner with the male clients. She also alleged that he openly told sexist jokes, intimated that she was pregnant and would soon be off the account, and kept characterizing her input as "That's what the lady thinks." In the investigation of this complaint, the manager admitted to making the statements, but claimed his conduct was not meant to offend anyone and that he surely would have stopped had he been informed at the time.

Practical Guidance

This situation cannot be solved with a slap on the wrist. An apology, a note to the file, and going forward with the planned promotion is not the answer. To promote this manager to a position of authority and leadership at this time would send the wrong message to all other managers and the entire workforce. The promotion should be delayed while the manager is required to undergo intensive sexual harassment training as part of the corrective action decision. Discipline in the form of a strong written warning should also be implemented. A manager should never be rewarded for inappropriate behavior, and the promotion should be reconsidered only after the company is convinced that the manager understands why his behavior is wrong and how to act appropriately in a business setting.

Notes

1. ___ U.S.___, 118 S. Ct. 2365 (1998).
2. Case No. 94-CIV-010871, Milwaukee Cty. Cir. Ct. (July 17, 1997).

CHAPTER 7

"Building an Olympic Team and Going for the Gold"
Sexual Harassment Training

I f you have an effective sexual harassment prevention policy that has been distributed to all employees and you consider your organization to be a good place where people are treated well, isn't that enough? The answer is no. A sexual harassment prevention policy, even when supported by good intentions and good people, is not sufficient. Fighting sexual harassment takes a combined team effort with both management and the rank and file. You need to make sure that everyone in the organization has the right tools and awareness to deal with sexual harassment head-on. To foster this team effort, you have a responsibility to provide training for all employees as a key component of maintaining a workplace free from sexual harassment.

Consider your policy as providing information on what to do when a sexual harassment issue arises. Training should supply the "how" in terms of promoting active support and compliance. As a manager, you alone cannot be the eyes and ears of the organization; nor would you want to be a corporate watchdog for bad behavior. Proper training on sexual harassment can help make all managers responsible and ensure accountability for following proper procedures with respect to all individuals.

This chapter defines what constitutes an effective training program, provides specifics on the contents of an effective training program, and addresses the myriad of issues that surround the training effort.

Test Your Knowledge

Most managers do not realize that they need an effective training program to educate the workforce and help model behaviors with respect to sexual harassment. Regardless of your current knowledge, the following true-and-false test highlights some important training issues; take the test, and record a T (for true) or an F (for false) before each statement. You may be surprised at how much you have already learned and can apply from reading the first six chapters of this book. After reading this final chapter, take the test again, and compare your answers to those provided at the end of the chapter.

True or False?

_____ **1.** Sexual harassment avoidance training is best accomplished by line managers.

_____ **2.** Training should emphasize the penalties associated with violating laws on sexual harassment, both to the company and to individual managers.

_____ **3.** Managers, supervisors, and employees all need the same training.

_____ **4.** The primary focus of the most effective training is on policy and behavioral guidelines.

_____ **5.** Training should be given to full-time employees only.

_____ **6.** Sophisticated executives don't need sexual harassment training.

_____ **7.** Training sessions for all new employees should not be held until the end of a probationary period, or until the new employee has become acclimated to the organization.

_____ **8.** The best way to document your training efforts is to keep a list of employees who attended each session.

_____ **9.** Training efforts are essential as part of a comprehensive sexual harassment prevention policy.

_____**10.** Training should be repeated annually.

The Importance of Sexual Harassment Training

An employer defending a sexual harassment case must first establish that it "exercised reasonable care to prevent and correct promptly any sexually harassing behavior" in the workplace. Having a comprehensive sexual harassment prevention policy with all the right buzzwords is the first step to show that you "exercised reasonable care." The second, and more important, step is to show that you did something more than put pen to paper. Implementing a mandatory sexual harassment training program for all employees is the only way to convince a judge, a jury, or your employees that the issue of sexual harassment is being addressed seriously. Anything less will greatly increase the risk of losing a case in court and losing the respect of your employees in the workforce.

Sexual Harassment Training Objectives

Obviously, you want to be sure that your training efforts are successful, and there are certain goals that need to be achieved, whether you work in a small office setting or for a Fortune 500 company

Total Workforce Awareness

The entire workforce needs to be trained on sexual harassment awareness issues in order to ensure that everyone has the same knowledge and understanding. Ignoring top management or other classifications of employees will result in inconsistent application of your sexual harassment prevention policy and lead to improper procedures.

Eradication of Sexual Harassment

A key objective of any sexual harassment training program is to eliminate sexual harassment from the workplace altogether and to provide instruction on the means by which employees can further this effort by properly observing all workplace conduct and reporting incidents of sexual harassment as soon as they occur.

Morale Improvement

A properly implemented sexual harassment training program can have an extremely positive effect on employee morale, provided that the focus is on communications and empowerment tools for employees. Fighting sexual harassment can be used as a method for improving teamwork and solidifying employees with a common goal. If employees perceive that the issue is important, they will have greater respect for the organization and feel that they are a big part of promoting the well-being of the entire workforce.

A successful training program will send a strong message to the entire workforce that the company is serious about sexual harassment and has the ability to handle such problems internally. It can promote trust and confidence in the company's abilities and the willingness of human resources professionals to listen. It will also increase the perception that the company is trying to be fair and objective and that it has a genuine interest in protecting employees from wrongful conduct.

Defense of Lawsuits

No company can escape the threat of a sexual harassment lawsuit. Providing effective and comprehensive sexual harassment training, however, can help the company mount a stronger defense if a lawsuit is filed. If training is required for all employees, it will be difficult for any court or jury to conclude that the company did not meet its legal responsibilities.

Behavioral Changes

One of the most important goals of any sexual harassment training program is to change inappropriate behaviors. Employees will never know how to act properly if they don't understand what proper behavior is. The training program needs to focus on behavioral changes by identifying specific behaviors that could pose a problem and teaching employees how to communicate differently.

The nature of communication will in fact change. Groups within the organization will begin to realize that it is no longer acceptable to be crude or boorish. Managers who once appeared insensitive to sexual harassment will recognize their past behavior and refrain from inappropriate conduct. You will also see managers stepping in to condemn behaviors that they previously ignored or even participated in. Employees will begin to censure each other, as peer pressure becomes a new means of enforcing the sexual harassment prevention policy. The organizational culture will eventually shift and new employees will hear from peers that "they don't do that here."

Preliminary Considerations for Effective Sexual Harassment Training

Once you recognize the necessity for training on sexual harassment, the question becomes how to do it most effectively. . Training efforts can range from a twenty-minute videotape to a full-day "live" session where the intricacies of sexual harassment and behavioral issues are addressed in addition to the legal issues. Before you attempt to choose a proper training program for your company, you need to ask some basic questions—for example:

- What is the right amount of training?

- What key points should be included?

- How many people should be trained at once?

- How often should the training be scheduled?

- Who should conduct the training?

- Who should be trained first?

- Should you start training in an area where you have had problems?

- Should different programs be offered for different segments of the workforce?

- Is there such a thing as training for a single "problem" employee?

Assessing Organizational Needs

Whether sexual harassment training is done by in-house managers or an outside consultant, it is extremely important to assess the actual needs of the organization and what you are trying to accomplish. Any experienced training consultant will begin this process by seeking to understand the particular workplace before offering solutions. In this regard, the following subjects will need to be covered with an outside consultant or by an in-house training staff.

Corporate Culture

What is the culture in the organization concerning sexual harassment? You need to determine if people are generally uninterested, if they have any awareness of the problem, or if most believe it is "no big deal." Without knowing how the existing corporate culture reacts to sexual harassment, it will be impossible to focus the training process in the right direction.

Are there any pending lawsuits or current complaints? This is very important to determine where the company is at the present time with respect to litigation and existing problems. A company that has had little exposure to the sexual harassment problem will require a much different training experience than a company that is finding itself in the midst of lawsuits.

Are any investigations in process? Investigation procedures will need to be addressed in any sexual harassment training program and knowledge about the company's existing practice in this regard is essential. A trainer needs to know how the company has been investigating sexual harassment complaints and if there are even any formal procedures in place if a complaint is lodged. Managers responsible for this task will most likely need special training on witness interviewing techniques, how to assess credibility, and how to organize an investigation.

Has there been an incident that is well known in the organization? This can range from outrageous behavior at yesterday's sales conference to a highly publicized situation that occurred some time ago. The conduct that caused such an incident may likely occur again and needs to be addressed in the training program. Employees will be more likely to identify with and understand inappropriate conduct when it has already occurred in their working environment. The trainer can use such examples to send a strong signal that offensive and otherwise problematic behavior must stop.

However, the trainer must be careful not to make any specific references to the incident itself or the individuals involved, so as not to embarrass anyone or breach the rules of confidentiality. The last thing a trainer should do is to put anyone on the spot or turn the program into a session where confessions about bad behavior are encouraged. Rather, the training program should use examples of inappropriate conduct as a catalyst for discussion and reinforcement of correct behaviors. Creating awareness about inappropriate conduct is the first step toward dealing with it in any sexual harassment training program.

Has there been recent publicity on sexual harassment concerning a competitor in the same industry? If so, this can also be a springboard for intelligent discussion about how sexual harassment can be prevented and handled. It can be used as an instructive tool with hypothetical questions, for example, "What if the same thing happened here?"

The main thing to remember is that sexual harassment training must never occur in a vacuum. "Canned" or generic training programs should be avoided at all costs. The program must be specifically tailored to the needs of the organization, and corporate culture and past history play a big role in planning an effective training program.

Management Attitudes

What message have employees been getting from the top? Are the CEO and upper management perceived as committed to preventing sexual harassment? How about other management staff? Do managers take the issue seriously, or do they tend to ignore or even participate in harassing behavior? You must assess the entire management staff, including personal beliefs and knowledge about the sexual harassment issue. In this way, you will have the ability to direct your training efforts toward dealing with management strengths and weaknesses.

Current Sexual Harassment Policies

What has the organization done to communicate its stand against sexual harassment, if anything, and how effective have those efforts been? Has a sexual harassment prevention policy been issued? Has any training been done to date? It is essential to study current policies and know exactly what has been communicated to employees thus far to determine if any of those communications are inaccurate, outdated, or misleading.

Special Problems

Is there an area of the company that would benefit most directly from sexual harassment training or an area where problems already exist? This includes areas where a previous incident was reported, where one gender predominates and hostility has been detected toward the inclusion of the opposite gender, where the historical norm has included sexual banter, and other areas of vulnerability such as small offices or areas with heavy client entertainment. Identifying these areas will help in designing a program to target specific issues and in determining where the training effort should be more strongly focused.

Employee Complement

How many employees need training? Where are they located? What shifts are they working? This number may be larger than you first imagined. Don't neglect to include part-timers, temporary workers, contract employees, people working from their homes, on-the-road salespeople, employees in remote locations and very small offices, and other employees who could be overlooked. Small groups of employees in remote locations will either need to travel to larger training sites or undergo different training methods, such as video and computer-based training. Additionally, employees working second or third shifts may require special provisions so that the program can be provided during working hours.

Accommodations

Are there any special requirements to ensure that training reaches all employees? Are there any disabled employees who will need to receive the training in a particular format? Are there any employees who do not speak or read English and will need a translation of the training materials and program? Identifying these needs early on will help provide the time to develop suitable accommodations.

Focus Groups

Collecting the right background information is the only way to determine and fully understand what type of training would be most suitable for your organization. Generally professional trainers want an in-depth look at the organization, including information on what the employees want to learn and what they think are the important issues. This information is usually derived from the use of focus groups.

These are diverse groups of employees with a mix of gender, age, tenure, and other classifications. They are brought together in groups of approximately eight to ten employees and asked to answer questions about their understanding of sexual harassment. Focus groups are also given an opportunity to indicate what they would like to learn about the subject and to suggest examples and situations that could be used as the basis for role playing, case scenarios, and other exercises.

A training facilitator should ask questions and record the responses. He or she should encourage participants to react to the responses of one another. All comments should be given equal treatment, and no member of the focus group should be criticized in any way or told that his or her responses are incorrect. There are, in fact, no wrong responses. The purpose of the focus group is only to obtain information about what subjects are important to people or need attention on the issue of sexual harassment.

For example, to test the issues on distribution and communication of a sexual harassment prevention policy, a training facilitator might ask, "Does the organization have a sexual harassment policy, and if so, have you read it?" Even though the organization may have distributed a policy and posted it, focus group participants can sometimes be unsure of its existence, or not remember reading it. All answers are necessary to identify the perceptions of focus group participants and thereby gauge the thoughts of the entire workforce. This information is valuable in constructing a training program specific to the needs of the organization. And the focus group format is extremely useful in building support and interest in the company's sexual harassment training efforts.

Deciding on the Best Training Format

In addition to doing all the homework about an organization, the training format must be decided. This involves making a determination of who will do the training and the best way to achieve the program goals.

Choosing the Best Trainer

You basically have two choices when deciding on the best trainer for your organization: use in-house personnel or hire an outside training consultant. If you decide to use your own management staff, you will probably need to train the trainers beforehand. Most large organizations can handle this, but many still prefer the second choice of using an outside consultant.

Using the services of an expert in the field will ensure that all employees are receiving the most comprehensive training available. There are many qualified professionals with well-tested experience in the design and delivery of sexual harassment training programs. Ask for referrals from other professionals, and carefully interview the candidates. Make sure to check references and find out how other organizations viewed the services and benefited. Finally, consider that sexual harassment training can be delivered by training professionals in conjunction with attorneys or human resources professionals, if appropriate for your organization.

Choosing the Best Methodology

The most effective and ideal learning situation is live, interactive, and skill-based training with examples and situations relevant to your organization. The best training format gives participants an opportunity to practice the skills they are learning. Training time for this type of program can range from a half-day to a full-day session and generally can accommodate up to twenty employees per session. Although there are many other formats, such as videos, lectures, and computer-based learning, the best methodology for conveying information is to use a live training facilitator who can hone in on individual skills and answer questions as they are asked.

You may find that the size of your organization, or its configuration, prohibits this type of training. What do you do if you have individual or small groups of employees to train, such as employees in remote locations, telecommuters, or new employees who missed the company-wide training program? In these cases, a sexual harassment video training program may suffice. However, this method will not deliver the impact and opportunity for skill development that is offered by a live, interactive training program.

Other practical considerations, such as the size of the group to be trained and the time frame for training, may also have an impact on the training methodology. When you have hundreds or thousands of people to train, a shorter two-hour format with the trainer appearing in person is still preferable to methods that remove the opportunity for direct interaction between the trainer and the participants.

Clearly, for maximum effectiveness you need more than a brief lecture on the basics of sexual harassment laws. Your program should provide an opportunity for interaction and offer role-playing exercises to help build awareness and sensitivity, and other skill-building exercises to teach participants how to address a sexual harassment problem, handle a complaint, and recognize inappropriate conduct as soon as it occurs. The more time that you can allot to training, the greater the opportunity you will have to get your message across and build the skills that will help employees fully understand all aspects of the sexual harassment issue.

Primary Topics for an Effective Sexual Harassment Training Program

Certain primary topics must be covered in any sexual harassment training program. Remember that your goal is not only to educate employees on the legal perils of sexual harassment, but also to train on appropriate and inappropriate behaviors and how to recognize and deal with a wide array of sexual harassment problems.

- Outline the legal definitions of sexual harassment with specific examples of quid pro quo and hostile-environment conduct.

- Stress the concept of "unwelcome" sexual advances. Discuss the potential of managers' being held personally liable for sexual harassment.

- Clarify the company's existing sexual harassment prevention policy, and offer suggestions for improvement. Review all other related organizational policies, such as those on grievance procedures, discipline, and company rules.

- Reinforce the organization's commitment and top management's support of maintaining a workplace free of sexual harassment. Highlight the meaning of *zero tolerance*, and identify inappropriate behaviors that should be banned even if they do not rise to the level of legal sexual harassment.

- Emphasize each individual employee's personal responsibility for following the organization's sexual harassment policy and maintaining a workplace free of sexual harassment.

- Explain retaliation issues, and give examples of how they can occur and how to avoid them.

- Heighten awareness and understanding of what is and what is not appropriate conduct through the use of role-playing exercises that build interpersonal sensitivity and awareness of how others wish to be treated and teach individuals how to monitor their own behavior. Underscore the importance of treating people in a respectful and professional manner.

- Use additional role-playing exercises to develop skills for identifying, preventing, and stopping sexually harassing behaviors and other inappropriate conduct at the workplace.

- Offer detailed guidance on how to avoid and how to handle being the target of sexual harassment.

- Carefully instruct on the proper procedures for reporting a sexual harassment complaint and a manager's responsibilities in this regard. Listening skills should be stressed. Ensure that participants are familiar with all of the organization's resources on this issue and how to access them for addressing questions and concerns and for reporting a complaint to the appropriate management officials.

- Clarify all sexual harassment complaint investigation procedures and the role of managers in investigating a complaint.

- Address corporate culture issues and how to change historical behaviors that may be inappropriate.

- Offer guidance for managers on how to address the issue of sexual harassment avoidance with subordinates through proper and effective communication skills.

- Improve techniques for implementing appropriate corrective action and how to treat all parties involved with respect and professionalism. Educate on the perils of managers' taking matters into their own hands.

Executive Endorsements

Training presents an ideal opportunity for the CEO or division executive to show his or her support and reinforce why the training is being conducted. The executive should personally open the program, stressing the values that support the training and the economic, ethical, legal, and business reasons for maintaining a workplace free of sexual harassment. The credibility of the executive will be enhanced if he or she has previously gone through the program and can endorse it as a positive experience. There is no better way to ensure that employees will take sexual harassment training seriously than to have support come right from the top.

Sample Training Outline

To help you create a sexual harassment training program in-house or to assist you with evaluating a program presented by a professional consultant, review the sample training outline in Exhibit 7-1. This particular program can be conducted in a one-half- or one-quarter-day session. Each training program section is followed by commentary on the significance of the section.

Exhibit 7-1. Sexual harassment awareness training program.

SEXUAL HARASSMENT AWARENESS TRAINING

I. PROGRAM INTRODUCTION

PROGRAM TOPICS

- Program Objectives
- Sexual Harassment From an Organizational Perspective
- Sexual Harassment in the U.S. Today: Assessment of Key Trends
- Where Are We Now?

Key Points

Before jumping into the law and the company's sexual harassment prevention policy, you need to state the program objectives and reinforce why the organization is concerned about sexual harassment. It is useful for participants to understand the widespread effect of the issue and the value that the organization can derive from maintaining a workplace free of sexual

Exhibit 7-1 (continued)

harassment, particularly from the standpoint of morale, employee retention, and productivity.

This opening is also a good place to mention current trends covering the issue, such as the rise in claims brought by men, the applicability of the law to gender-based harassment, e-mail issues, and other items currently in the news. You will want to clarify that legal liability may extend (depending on local and state laws) to individual supervisors.

II. CLARIFYING THE LAW AND THE SEXUAL HARASSMENT POLICY

- EEOC Guidelines—Definition of Sexual Harassment
- Quid Pro Quo Sexual Harassment
- Is This Conduct Lawful?
- Hostile Work Environment Sexual Harassment
- Clarifying the Concept of "Unwelcome" Sexual Advances
- Exercise: Raising Awareness About Unwelcome Behavior
- Review of the Sexual Harassment Policy
- Review of the Organization's Stand Against Retaliation
- Exercise: Putting Your Knowledge to the Test
- Organizational Initiatives: Information, Role of Human Resources, Support for Maintaining a Workplace Free of Sexual Harassment

Key Points

The EEOC Guidelines, the definition of sexual harassment, and your organization's policy must be reviewed in its entirety, with care taken to explain both quid pro quo and hostile work environment sexual harassment with examples. It is also useful to provide exercises to allow participants to see how behaviors they may view as appropriate may be perceived as unwelcome by their peers. Participants should learn to avoid all improper conduct even if it may not rise to the level of sexual harassment in the legal sense. The touchstone for this discussion is to encourage professional and businesslike conduct at all times.

When clarifying the organization's sexual harassment prevention policy, you should read the policy aloud and answer all questions about it. The key aspects of the policy should be stressed: the organization's firm commitment to eliminating sexual harassment from the workplace (zero tolerance), freedom from retaliation, how to report a complaint, handling investigations, and taking appropriate corrective action. The fact that employees can report a problem to one of several individuals without the need to speak first to their direct supervisor should also be stressed.

This section of the program is also a good place to introduce the concept of the "extended workplace." Employees must understand that the law also covers their behavior when interacting with other employees in venues outside the four walls of the office. The "workplace" can include interactions with vendors and customers, social and entertainment-oriented settings, trade shows, conventions, business trips, and a host of other activities that occur away from the workplace.

III. RAISING AWARENESS ABOUT SEXUAL HARASSMENT
- Understanding Sexual Harassment in a Broader Context: Relations Between People in the Workplace
- Developing Sensitivity to How Your Actions Are Perceived
- Exercise: How Attitudes and Perceptions Affect Behavior
- Treating People With Dignity and Respect

Key Points

The purpose of this section is to build sensitivity to the feelings and perceptions of others and to guide employees to treat others the way they believe they should be treated. You may recall from Chapter 3, which addressed your attitudes and conduct, that practicing the "golden rule" of doing unto others as you would have others do unto you is not always appropriate when sexual harassment is the issue. Remember that conduct that you may find acceptable may have exactly the opposite effect on someone else. This section of the training program should stress this point. It should also address some of the basic attitudes and assumptions that can cause sexual harassment accusations. It invites self-examination and builds awareness of the idea that even well-intentioned or nonmalicious communication can have dire consequences. The key is to know how to avoid sexually harassing behaviors.

IV. YOUR PERSONAL RESPONSIBILITY FOR MAINTAINING A WORKPLACE FREE FROM SEXUAL HARASSMENT
- What Is Your Responsibility?
- Respecting the Rights of Others
- Monitoring Your Own Behavior
- Quick Rules for the Workplace: Creating the Right Environment to Avoid Sexual Harassment

Exhibit 7-1 (continued)
Key Points

This section reinforces personal responsibility for following company policies on sexual harassment or otherwise and gives guidance on how to monitor one's own behavior. The objective is to empower all employees to be aware of their own conduct, to make changes as needed, and to catch and immediately correct any missteps as they occur.

V. HOW TO DEAL WITH SEXUAL HARASSMENT

- The Proactive Approach: How to Avoid Being Sexually Harassed
- Knowing Your Options: Steps to Follow If You Are Sexually Harassed
- You Are Encouraged to Take Action
- Effective Ways for Dealing With Unwelcome Conduct
- Role Play: Communicating With a Peer About Unwelcome Behavior
- How to Take a Complaint Forward

Key Points

This section empowers participants to take action if they feel they have been harassed, either by addressing the person who is bothering them or by bringing it to the attention of their manager or another individual who is designated to hear complaints. The role play is an effective means of building the skills necessary to confront an alleged harasser directly. This section should also clearly define how internal complaints will be handled in terms of expediency, methodology, and confidentiality.

VI. REINFORCING THE COMMITMENT TO MAINTAIN A WORKPLACE FREE OF SEXUAL HARASSMENT

- The Organization's Commitment to You
- Final Questions and Answers

Key Points

This is the final section in the program for nonmanagerial employees. Supervisors and managers will need one more essential element for their training, which follows in the section below. This final employee section should include a review of the steps the organization has taken to maintain a workplace free of sexual harassment, including training, policy, and complaint procedure. This is followed by a Q&A session so that employees can ask their final questions. You can stimulate the Q&A session by developing some questions of your own that you think are important.

Answers to "Test Your Knowledge"

VII. MANAGER RESPONSIBILITIES FOR DEALING WITH SEXUAL HARASSMENT

- How to Take a Proactive View Toward Preventing Sexual Harassment
- Setting the Tone for a Safe Environment: Successfully Communicating With Employees About Sexual Harassment
- Role Play: How to Communicate About Sexual Harassment With Employees in a Constructive Way
- Gaining Commitment From Employees
- The Role of Human Resources
- How to Manage a Complaint

Key Points

This section gives managers a clear direction for their critical role in preventing sexual harassment and in dealing with complaints. Since no one individual, whether the CEO or the head of human resources, can be the eyes and ears of the organization or personally ensure that sexual harassment does not occur, this accountability logically resides with supervisors and managers within their own area. A role play provides skill practice in how to spot and resolve problems before they give rise to actual complaints. Supervisors and managers also need to learn how to demonstrate leadership on this issue by modeling correct behaviors, setting the right tone of zero tolerance in their area, communicating about sexual harassment in a positive way, and taking the right actions to recognize and respond to complaints.

---

1. *Sexual harassment avoidance training is best accomplished by line managers.*

FALSE. Generally line managers, unless they have been trained themselves, do not have the subject matter expertise and training presentation skills required to make an effective delivery. Additionally, sexual harassment training requires sensitivity to the issue and the ability to handle challenges and skepticism from participants. Usually it is best to engage a training expert in this area who can convey the subject matter and has the ability to facilitate discussion and interaction among participants, so real learning may occur.

2. Training should emphasize the penalties associated with violating laws on sexual harassment, to both the company and individual managers.

FALSE. Although citing penalties is important, the main thrust of the training program should be to emphasize the commitment of the organization to provide a workplace free of sexual harassment and the responsibilities of every employee to make that a reality.

3. Managers, supervisors, and employees all need the same training.

FALSE. This is a trick question. Although all employees need the basics in understanding and avoiding sexual harassment, and knowing how to report a problem, managers and supervisors need additional training in their specific responsibilities in creating the right atmosphere, modeling correct behaviors, managing complaints, and being mindful of the behaviors that could create a quid pro quo sexual harassment accusation.

4. The primary focus of the most effective training is on policy and behavioral guidelines.

FALSE. The most effective training includes much more than policy and behavioral guidelines; it provides an opportunity for participants to build skills in addressing sexual harassment and helps managers to practice how to respond. Building these skills involves experiential exercises such as role plays.

5. Training should be given to full-time employees only.

FALSE. Every employee must receive training. This includes part-time employees, temporary employees, contract employees, and employees who are on the road.

6. Sophisticated executives don't need sexual harassment training.

FALSE. This may be one of the great myths. Executives, including the CEO and COO in particular, must be able to "walk the talk." Without proper training they cannot be expected to fulfill their important role for modeling correct behaviors, setting the right tone for taking the matter seriously, and reinforcing the zero tolerance policy.

7. *Training sessions for all new employees should not be held until the end of a probationary period, or until the new employee has become acclimated to the organization.*

FALSE. All new employees should receive training as part of their orientation to the organization. It is important to convey what the organization expects in terms of behavior and policy compliance from the start of the employment relationship and react to a potential problem that was caused by a new employee who didn't know or understand the rules.

8. *The best way to document training efforts is to keep a list of employees who attended each session.*

FALSE. Documentation of training program attendance is best accomplished by having each participant personally sign out at the end of the training session, indicating they have completed the training program. A list of program attendees, without their signatures, is less effective in proving who actually completed the training.

9. *Training efforts are essential as part of a comprehensive sexual harassment prevention policy.*

TRUE. Having a sexual harassment policy is not a sufficient deterrent to sexual harassment on either a legal or a practical basis. Although employees may read the policy, understanding it on a practical basis, knowing how to comply with it, developing greater awareness and sensitivity to others, and knowing how to deal with problems or potential problems require training in an interactive format, where questions can be asked and answered and skills can be developed.

10. *Training should be repeated annually.*

TRUE. For training to be effective, it needs to be repeated. A regular schedule of training should be established to ensure that employees are being trained once a year. As new case law develops and as organizations revise and tighten their sexual harassment avoidance polices, new behavioral and compliance expectations need to be communicated through training.

Case Scenarios and Practical Guidance for the Real World

Scenario A

You recently attended a meeting of managers where the company's sexual harassment prevention policy was discussed. Several managers thought the whole issue was nonsense. Others felt that common sense was enough of a guide to keep everyone out of trouble.

Practical Guidance

Discussion alone is not the best tool for changing behavior and creating awareness. You need training support to reach employees on different levels, create awareness, and reinforce the necessity of compliance.

Scenario B

The management committee has rejected the idea of sexual harassment avoidance training. They feel they are above it. Some of the worst offenders, however, sit on the committee.

Practical Guidance

Your management committee, along with the CEO, will set the tone for behavior throughout the organization. If they cannot "walk the talk," no one will think that the organization takes the issue of sexual harassment seriously. Training for this group is essential. Do not reduce training to a thirty-minute briefing. Executives should have in-depth interactive training. A high place on the organizational chart does not produce automatic sensitivity or insight into sexually harassing behaviors or how to deal with the issue. Executives sometimes need more sensitivity and awareness training than the rank and file because of their highly visible leadership role.

Scenario C

During a sexual harassment training session, one of the employees reveals that she is having a problem with her manager. He apparently talks in a suggestive manner and constantly comments on the "firmness" of her body.

Practical Guidance

An experienced sexual harassment trainer should recognize and tell the participants that the training environment is not the appropriate place to report a claim of sexual harassment and that the allegations should be immediately brought to the attention of senior management. However, the situation will give the trainer an opportunity to educate the group on proper complaint procedures and the fact that complaints can arise anywhere. The trainer should also report the incident to senior management after the session.

Scenario D

During a sexual harassment training session, managers are instructed on the role of the company's human resources department in handling investigations of sexual harassment complaints. Based on some of their experiences, many of the managers raise serious concerns about the ability of that department to be organized and maintain the confidentiality of such claims. Another manager is very concerned about his own personal liability if he reports a complaint and the human resources department fails to take prompt action.

Practical Guidance

This scenario highlights the need for the comprehensive and effective training of senior management officials who will be responsible for the complaint, investigation, and corrective action procedures relating to sexual harassment. The procedures must be covered in detail, with emphasis on methods for maintaining confidentiality, objectivity, and credibility through swift and complete action. Training on the potential of personal liability for managers must also be included in every management training session. The trainer should cover the serious dangers of participants taking matters into their own hands and trying to resolve a sexual harassment claim without the appropriate members of a management team.

Additionally, if managers or other employees do not have faith in the human resources department, such a serious issue needs to be addressed independently from the sexual harassment training program. The trainer should immediately report the employees' concerns to senior management so that constructive action to remedy the situation can begin. Senior management must confirm that the human resources department is properly following up on sexual harassment complaints and communicating about its actions to line managers who have referred the complaints.

Index

vigilante efforts involving, 108
credibility
    of "credibility problem" employees,
        109–110, 119
    in investigation process, 135, 136,
        137, 141, 148–149, 154
cultural differences, 37–38
customers
    biases toward large, 84–85
    entertaining, 82–83, 95
    sexual harassment by, 26–27, 40,
        46–47, 58, 78–79, 82–83, 90, 94,
        100, 121
    and stereotypical beliefs about
        women, 78–79, 90

"delayed reaction" employees, taking
    complaints from, 110–113
dignity, 85–86
"direct hit" complaints, 99–100
direct supervisors
    complaint filing with, 51, 52, 65, 74
    sexual harassment by, 111–112,
        141, 152
discipline for harassers, 167–175
    factors determining level of, 54–55,
        169
    forms of, 168–169
    past disciplinary record and, 183
    progressive, 167–169
dress, 80

EEOC v. General Motors Corp., 107
Ellerth, Kimberly, 19–20, 172–173
e-mail, 102
embarrassed employees, taking com-
    plaints from, 106
embarrassing questions, 138
employee handbooks, 57
employment discrimination
    EEOC Guidelines, 5–11, 18–19
    sexual harassment as, 1–2, 4–5, 46
Equal Employment Opportunity
    Commission (EEOC)
    Guidelines, 4–11
    complaints and, 97, 107, 119

"negligence" standard, 25
    sex discrimination and, 5–11,
        18–19
    "WAR" requirements for
        prevention policy, 43–44
evidence, in investigations, 132–133,
    134, 147–148, 174
executives, attitudes about sexual
    harassment, 199, 204, 206
eye contact, 36, 72

facial expression, importance of
    when taking complaints, 103
fairness, of investigators, 128
false accusations, 77, 165–166, 182
Faragher, Beth Ann, 20–23, 43, 111
Faragher v. City of Boca Raton, 19,
    20–23, 25, 43, 56, 111, 126
favoritism, 84–85
flirting, 39, 92–93, 121–122
focus groups, 194–195
friendliness, 80–81
friendship
    between complainant and
        harasser, 108–109
    between manager and harasser,
        120–121
funny stories, 28–29

general agency principles of law, 22
globalization trend, 37–38
gossip, 29, 138, 147, 153
graffiti, sexual, 47, 102
graphic sexual materials, 30–31, 36,
    37, 47, 76
grievance procedures, 52, 107

handbooks, employee, 57
harassers
    corrective action for, 54–55, 66–67,
        167–175, 177
    fighting back by, 178–179
    ten most dangerous types of, 28–31
"hard to get," playing, 80
Hardy, Charles, 16–17
Harris, Teresa, 16–17